Life is hard
  and unfair
    and painful
      and perplexing . . .

What are students to do?

... with friends who
share a biblical worldview.

• Wrestle through how to live
out God's truth.

DOWNLOAD YOUR
FREE GUIDE TO:
• Share with one another
• Learn what God's Word says
• Help each other figure it out
• Hold each other accountable
• Pray for one another
• And watch God work!

IF ANY OF YOU LACKS
WISDOM, LET HIM ASK
OF GOD, WHO GIVES
TO ALL LIBERALLY
AND WITHOUT
REPROACH, AND IT
WILL BE GIVEN TO HIM.
—JAMES 1:5

GRAB A GROUP
talk it out—live it out

#criticalissues

#absoluteanswers

$\{$ **SOLUTIONS FOR STUDENTS** $\}$

DR. JAY STRACK
GENERAL EDITOR

THOMAS NELSON
Since 1798

A Division of Thomas Nelson Publishers

NASHVILLE   DALLAS   MEXICO CITY   RIO DE JANEIRO

Published in Nashville, Tennessee, by Thomas Nelson. Thomas Nelson is a registered trademark of Thomas Nelson, Inc.

Thomas Nelson, Inc., titles may be purchased in bulk for educational, business, fund-raising, or sales promotional use. For information, please e-mail SpecialMarkets@ThomasNelson.com.

Unless otherwise noted, Scripture quotations are taken from THE NEW KING JAMES VERSION. © 1982 by Thomas Nelson, Inc. Used by permission. All rights reserved.

Scripture quotations marked ESV are from THE ENGLISH STANDARD VERSION. © 2001 by Crossway Bibles, a division of Good News Publishers.

Scripture quotations marked NLT are from *Holy Bible*, New Living Translation. © 1996. Used by permission of Tyndale House Publishers, Inc., Wheaton, Illinois 60189. All rights reserved.

Scripture quotations marked NASB are from NEW AMERICAN STANDARD BIBLE®, © The Lockman Foundation 1960, 1962, 1963, 1968, 1971, 1972, 1973, 1975, 1977, 1995. Used by permission.

Scripture quotations marked NIV are from the Holy Bible, New International Version®, NIV®. Copyright © 1973, 1978, 1984 by Biblica, Inc™. Used by permission of Zondervan. All rights reserved worldwide. www.zondervan.com.

Scripture quotations marked HCSB are from *Holman Christian Standard Bible*. © 1999, 2000, 2002, 2003 by Holman Bible Publishers, Nashville, Tennessee. All rights reserved.

Scripture quotations marked TLB are from *The Living Bible*. © 1971. Used by permission of Tyndale House Publishers, Inc., Wheaton, Illinois 60189. All rights reserved.

Scripture quotations marked MSG are from *The Message* by Eugene H. Peterson. © 1993, 1994, 1995, 1996, 2000. Used by permission of NavPress Publishing Group. All rights reserved.

Scripture quotations marked NCV are from New Century Version®. © 2005 by Thomas Nelson, Inc. Used by permission. All rights reserved.

Scripture quotations marked RSV are from REVISED STANDARD VERSION of the Bible. © 1946, 1952, 1971, 1973 by the Division of Christian Education of the National Council of the Churches of Christ in the U.S.A. Used by permission.

Scripture quotations marked KJV are from the King James Version.

ISBN-13: 978-1-4003-7512-7

Printed in the United States of America

13 14 15 16 17 WOR 6 5 4 3 2 1

#contents

#preface

Since the dawn of the early church, Christians have gathered to worship Jesus Christ, the One who freely gave His life that we might know Him in an intimate, personal relationship. We were created to worship Him in earnest prayer, to fellowship and encourage one another, and to live according to the Word of God. By God's grace, the result would be a strong and unified body of believers inspired to go confidently out into the world as servant leaders who share the good news and offer a tangible expression of love through missions.

Sadly, many Christians find themselves disconnected from fellow believers, if not from God Himself; questioning the fundamental doctrines of the faith; and timid in their understanding of a Christian worldview. This uncertainty is understandable given the volume of chatter and the variety of opinions floating through the universe on a daily basis. Who is right? There is absolutely no question: the Word of God is truth, and this will not change regardless of the culture's voices.

Student Leadership University was founded on this scripture: "Sanctify the Lord God in your hearts, and always be ready to give a defense to everyone who asks you a reason for the hope that is in you, with meekness and fear" (1 Peter 3:15). SLU exists to train students how to be confident in their beliefs and able to clearly articulate why they believe what they do. Wanting every person to have this kind of confidence, we set out with much prayer and deliberation to put together this collaborative effort of *#CriticalIssues and #AbsoluteAnswers.*

If you combine all of the contributors' impressive resumes and lifetime accomplishments, you have over two hundred years of experience at

1

your fingertips. Among the writers are seminary presidents and professors, dedicated educators, and some of the most experienced and effective youth ministers on the planet. What you have in your hands is a great work, written by those who understand the culture and language of your generation and who are dedicated to providing biblical clarity about critical issues. More importantly, they know that the Scriptures are able to make us "wise unto salvation" as we think deeply and walk worthy of our calling (2 Timothy 3:15 KJV). While this book is intentionally directed to students, it is also intended to be a tool for every pastor, educator, youth worker, parent, and counselor who cares about the youth of this nation and this planet.

In today's fog of uncertainty, relativism, and revisionists, we need clear and concise answers. The Scripture says, "For if the trumpet makes an uncertain sound, who will prepare for battle?" (1 Corinthians 14:8). It seems that almost every day the trumpet is playing "Taps" for this generation. It is our collective prayer that, after reading these #CriticalIssues and the #AbsoluteAnswers, both students and adults will begin to confidently sound forth "Reveille" in a call to this generation to prepare to win the battles that lie ahead.

> That the generation to come might know [God's teaching and law], the children who would be born, that they may arise and declare them to their children, that they may set their hope in God, and not forget the works of God, but keep His commandments. (Psalm 78:6–7)

DR. JAY STRACK

FOUNDER AND PRESIDENT,

STUDENT LEADERSHIP UNIVERSITY

www.studentleadership.net

#identity

Finding Your Pace

BROOKE COONEY
Calvary Baptist Church, Clearwater, FL

At some point during every semester in elementary school, we were given the President's Physical Fitness Test. Every time I anxiously awaited my turn, and every time I hoped that this run would be different. As an asthmatic, I actually hoped that not every lap would end with my dropping out early, gasping for air while inhaling a few puffs of my inhaler, and subsequently receiving comfort from the teacher. (Yes, that was embarrassing.) I never did complete one physical fitness test at a sprint, so I effectively labeled myself "not a runner" and avoided running altogether.

Now, a few decades later, I run 5Ks weekly. What changed? Well, as I have grown, the signs of asthma have primarily diminished. I started running short spurts with friends. Over time I gained confidence that I could set and meet my next running goal. I was spurred on by my husband and motivated by friends' successes.

Developing a godly character is much like training to run a race. Virtuous character is formed one deliberate and obedient step at a time. Even dramatic conversions to Christianity, like Paul's, result in Christlike character only with discipline and obedience to the Scriptures.

> Do you not know that in a race all the runners run, but only one receives the prize? So run that you may obtain it. Every athlete exercises self-control in all things. They do it to receive a perishable wreath, but we an imperishable. So I do not run aimlessly; I do not box as one beating the air. But I discipline my body and keep it under control, lest after preaching to others I myself should be disqualified. (1 Corinthians 9:24–27 ESV)

Paul, like us, had the opportunity to make ungodly, unwise decisions that would be pleasurable or lucrative in the moment but potentially have devastating consequences for generations to come. Our obedience and our disobedience will either profit us or cost us, *as well as* all the people we influence. So Paul resolved to discipline his body and be master over it lest he weaken both his communion with God and his witness. He chose to pursue godly character for the furtherance of the gospel and the growth of his relationship with Christ. Paul did not become a pillar of the faith at his point of conversion, but as he lived in obedience to Christ's commands.

In contrast to Paul is Samson. Although Samson was called and anointed by God, his life illustrates the cost of being trapped by temporary pleasures and neglecting character development (Judges 13:5; 16). Samson was physically strong but tragically weak in self-discipline, unable to overcome both his temper and his desire for beautiful women. Samson's lust cost him his sight, his freedom, his life. He was physically strengthened by the Holy Spirit to carry out God's will against His enemies, but Samson did not pursue strength of character. He did not clear the hurdle of lust, that part of him that said, "I want that—and I want it now!"

Samson's downfall was beautiful women, but it can easily be money, status, or power. Giving in to the voracious hunger of our sinful heart will cost us our freedom (Romans 6:6–7). So how do we lay off the sin that clings to us (Hebrews 12:1) and instead pursue a Christlike character? Running that race takes the daily renewal of our minds through the Word, prayer, and fellowship with believers.

Christlike character develops with exposure to the Word of God:

> How can a young man keep his way pure? By guarding it according to your word. With my whole heart I seek you; let me not wander from your commandments! . . . I have chosen the way of faithfulness; I set your rules before me. I cling to your testimonies, O Lord; let me not be put to shame! I will run in the way of your commandments when you enlarge my heart! (Psalm 119:9–10, 30–32 ESV)

Knowing **God's Word** and following His commandments will build our character and strengthen our spiritual muscles so we avoid becoming prey for the devil. Just as lions pursue the weakest of their targeted prey, we are easy targets for the pseudo-lion, the devil (1 Peter 5:8), when we neglect character development, when we don't make time for the reading, study, and memorization of Scripture. When we pore over God's Word daily, though, we pace ourselves with the Alpha Lion, the Lion of the tribe of Judah (Revelation 5:5).

Prayer is the next step. We should pray about our moral weaknesses, first acknowledging them before God and then seeking His strength and His truth. Christ, the Word made flesh, was diligent in prayer up to the very hour when He was betrayed. Fully God and fully man, Jesus knew what obedience would cost Him, yet still He prayed for God's will to be done (Luke 22:39–46).

Finally, character is influenced by the **company** we keep. Growing spiritually in a youth group and finding adult leaders to mentor and encourage faithfulness to God is key to running a good race. We find encouragement to stay the course of Christ in His body, the church (Hebrews 10:24–25). We need to avoid making excuses about how running the race with others slows us down.

These days I look forward to running. I didn't start with any real desire to run, but with time and training, I now run with both perseverance and pleasure. For the utmost pursuit of Christlike character, we must press on. We must forget the failures *and* the successes of the past and run with obedient perseverance the race marked out for today (Hebrews 12:1–3). When we do so, we will look back at the end of our lives and see that running the race in obedience to Christ resulted in godly character that brought Him glory.

> For the utmost pursuit of Christlike character, we must press on. >

Living in a World That Demands Perfection

JEREMY NOTTINGHAM
First Baptist Church, Broken Arrow, OK

Coaches want touchdowns, goals, and home runs. Teachers want As and 4.0s. Band directors want to win national band competitions. Colleges want perfect ACT scores and tons of extracurricular activities. Parents want scholarships. Employers want lots of effort. Youth pastors want commitment to church events and godly lifestyles. When did the life of a teenager become so busy, demanding, and challenging? Do you ever just want to scream? The demands have continued to mount over the years, and they show no signs of letting up. In fact, it appears that the only way to make it in life is to fall in step with every demand and do whatever it takes.

Practice makes perfect is what students have always been told. We pretty much realize that perfection is impossible, but—and I'm not telling you anything you don't already know—teens are forced to pursue perfection like never before. Some of you have band practice or football practice for hours in the killer heat of August. It has become a job to many of you, and your love for the music or the game slowly fades as you pursue your goal of perfection. Others of you stay up late working on homework trying to keep your GPA up so you can get into a good college—or any college, for that matter! Colleges have put the pressure on potential students because of limited space. So the pursuit of high ACT scores to land the right school and a good scholarship has meant an increase in the academic workload.

The danger we find in this fast-paced and demanding lifestyle is the breakdown of a teenager's spiritual life. Unfortunately, because of the craziness of schedules and demands, you young people often have to let something go. Usually, when the pressure mounts, the spiritual life will be the first to go.

After all, you teenagers generally don't get graded on how you're doing spiritually, and colleges aren't asking how many quiet times you had in the past year. So the pressure to be perfect in academics, sports, and fine arts is, in my opinion, one of the leading causes in the spiritual decline on an individual and national basis.

Thom S. Rainer and Jess W. Rainer have taken a careful look at your Millennial generation. Today's teens are on the back end of this generation, but the Rainers have great insight into the spirituality of this group. Their research unveiled sobering statistics: "The shocking reality for us is that only 13 percent of the Millennials considered any type of spirituality to be important in their lives."[1] If the pressure and priorities don't change, this astounding and frightening statistic will only get worse. The Rainers also learned that when Millennials were asked if Jesus was the only way to heaven, "only 31 percent strongly agree with this belief. The rest have a tepid belief in the doctrine, or they disagree with it altogether."[2] Almost three out of four in your generation do not know or believe in the truth of Jesus Christ. Adults who are coaches, teachers, parents, band directors, youth pastors, and I'm sure you can add to the list—all of us need to remember that your spiritual life is more important than where you get into school and where you could play soccer on a scholarship.

So, how can you navigate through this world of high expectations remembering that your spiritual life is more important than anything else—and living that way? Matthew 6:19–21 says, "Do not lay up for yourselves treasures on earth, where moth and rust destroy and where thieves break in and steal; but lay up for yourselves treasures in heaven, where neither moth nor rust destroys and where thieves do not break in and steal. For where your treasure is, there your heart will be also." Now, I'm not at all suggesting that you throw in the towel with either academics or athletics. Not at all! Those are extremely important, but your relationship with Christ is even more important—far more important—than these things. Colossians 3:2 says, "Set your mind on things above, not on things on the earth." Every effort of study or athletics should be in an effort to bring glory to God and a pursuit of the things that matter in eternity.

So I invite you—I challenge you—to make a stand and a change. Seek Christ first in all you do and let everything else fall into place after that. Don't let the pressures of life and the demands of perfection interfere with or even derail your walk with Jesus. He must be first in everything you do, because He truly is the Fullness of Life.

> Every effort of study or athletics should be in an effort to bring glory to God. **>**

What We Should Say to Our Reflection

BROOKE COONEY
Calvary Baptist Church, Clearwater, FL

You formed my inward parts; you knitted me together in my mother's womb. I praise you, for I am fearfully and wonderfully made. Wonderful are your works; my soul knows it very well.

—Psalm 139:13–14 ESV

As Christ followers, we say that we believe the Bible is God's inerrant Word. Yet when our stomachs are bloated, our biceps too small, our curves in all the "wrong" places, or our best is less than someone else's, we waver. At moments like those, we often choose to exchange the truth of God's Word for the lie "I am not wonderfully made."

We all fall into the sin of comparison (2 Corinthians 10:12, 18). In a world that broadcasts inaccurate messages of air-brushed beauty, we let God's idea of true beauty be overruled by the idol of our culture's standards (1 Peter 3:4).

God says that we are created in His image "to do good works, which [He] prepared in advance for us to do" (Ephesians 2:10 NIV). We are created for a purpose, and that purpose is forgotten when we view ourselves through the eyes of fallen man, think on temporary things, or ponder imagined realities.

When Samuel was sent to the house of Jesse to anoint Israel's next king, he was looking through the lens of man, not God's. Samuel would have anointed the wrong man had God not spoken these words:

> Do not look at his appearance or at his physical stature, because I have refused him. For the Lord does not see as man sees; for man looks at the outward appearance, but the Lord looks at the heart. (1 Samuel 16:7)

God looks at what cannot be seen with even the latest medical technology: the heart and soul of man. The heart is a creation that can only be perceived by an intimate knowing, and God knows us in the most intimate way. On that basis He declares us a wonderful work:

> God said, "Let Us make man in Our image, according to Our likeness." . . . Then God saw everything that He had made, and indeed it was very good. (Genesis 1:26, 31)

> O Lord, You have searched me and known me. You know my sitting down and my rising up; You understand my thought afar off. You comprehend my path and my lying down, and are acquainted with all my ways. (Psalm 139:1–3)

In order for us to bring God glory, we must focus on the facts and honor no other god. In today's society, however, we often bow down to the gods of fame, beauty, popularity, power, and success. This is called *humanism* and is defined as "the focusing of energy and attention to humankind and not looking for help or salvation from any deity."[1]

We are duped into thinking that if we look, eat, think, and act in certain ways, we can fulfill the longing in our hearts as well as save ourselves from ourselves. This is not what God's Word teaches:

> **The Bible teaches God-confidence. >**

> Not that we are to classify or compare ourselves with some of those who are commending themselves. But when they measure themselves by one another and compare themselves with one another, they are without understanding. . . . For it is not the one who commends himself who is approved, but the one whom the Lord commends. (2 Corinthians 10:12, 18 esv)

Furthermore, worldly wisdom teaches self-confidence, but the Bible teaches God-confidence:

> We have such trust through Christ toward God. Not that we are sufficient of ourselves to think of anything as being from ourselves, but *our sufficiency is from God.* (2 Corinthians 3:4–5, emphasis added)

> *God gave us* a spirit not of fear but of power and love and self-control. (2 Timothy 1:7 ESV, emphasis added)

Self-esteem, self-confidence, and acceptance of oneself—all this is false confidence if it is not attached to God-confidence.

At the moment of our salvation, God gave us His Holy Spirit, who equips us with God's power that is sufficient for all things. Reading God's Word enables the Holy Spirit to transform our minds and conform our actions to that of Christ Jesus. Through this process we become competent ministers of the gospel of Christ. God has designed good works for us to do with our physical bodies, and once we engage in that work as ministers of Christ, we transfer our thinking to the eternal and lay aside the consuming burdensome thoughts of self (Romans 12:1–2). We then live in the knowledge that this world is our temporary home.

Next, living with a heavenly kingdom in mind, we replace the negative thoughts in our mind with the mind of Christ. We change our inner dialogue, our self-talk.

Self-talk is what we say about ourselves in our minds. Oftentimes our self-talk consists of negative statements like "I never do _____ right" and "I always mess _____ up." The Bible clearly teaches that we should fill our mind with what is honorable, just, pure, lovely, commendable, excellent, or worthy of praise (Philippians 4:8). These thoughts lead to a peaceful spirit that

God calls us to pursue (1 Peter 3:11) while simultaneously helping us "abstain from every form of evil" in the present age (1 Thessalonians 5:22).

Shifting our focus from our outward appearance to the inward quality of our heart, basing our self-confidence on God-confidence, and transforming our self-talk to align with the truth of Scripture are steps we need to take toward living with godly self-esteem. Then, when we look in the mirror, may we affirm the truths of God: we are wonderfully made in His image for His kingdom's work.

Taking Responsibility for YOU!

CHUCK ALLEN
Sugar Hill Church, Sugar Hill, GA

I recall watching General Norman Schwarzkopf in a battlefield briefing during Operation Desert Storm when he said, "To win this war, our goal isn't to fix blame, but rather to fix problems." When General Schwarzkopf said that, I immediately recalled the time my high school baseball team was playing for the state championship. Things weren't going our way, and the dugout was full of whiners, gripers, and excuses as to why we weren't "getting it done." Our coach sat us all down, took a deep breath, and in terms that were Waterford-crystal clear told us that champions are filled with courage, not excuses.

I vividly remember blaming my older sister for a stupid decision I made. Upon learning the truth of the situation, my mother taught me a great lesson, and that lesson has helped shape my life, my family, my career, and my ministry. Mom said this: "Never trust a whiner and never become a whiner. They turn rights into wrongs and wrongs into resentment."

These three examples shout to us that the world needs young champions to step up and lead, not just follow; to fix problems, not fix blame; to right the world rather than find more wrong.

So, just how do we keep from falling into the trap of the blame game? Well, I'm glad you asked. First, always remember that your character, not your achievements, will forever measure you. As a result, being a person of godly character is essential. Now let me offer you *four* cornerstones of character that can help you always be the person who fixes problems rather than fixes blame.

1. DON'T BE "THAT GUY"

Relationships. The human experience is all about relationships. God built us to be in relationship with others and especially in a healthy relationship with Him. In fact, a healthy relationship with Jesus is the key to being in right relationships with those around you. (A relationship with Jesus is also the key to the next three cornerstones.) And because nobody likes being blamed and nobody trusts a person who is doing the blaming, blame can undermine relationships. People place their trust in one another, and that trust is proven or ruined by how we deal with problems, conflicts, and everyday interactions. Folks trust you when you're competent, when you know what you're doing, but people *fully* trust you when they can trust your character. So choose to be The Man, not That Guy.

2. GET A HEART TRANSPLANT

The second critical cornerstone to taking responsibility and leaving an imprint of excellence is *purity*. Titus 1:15–16 says this: "To the pure all things are pure, but to those who are defiled and unbelieving nothing is pure; but even their mind and conscience are defiled. They profess to know God, but in works they deny Him, being abominable, disobedient, and disqualified for every good work." In other words, what you do in word and in action reveals your heart. A pure heart takes personal responsibility while a heart of deceit is always looking to play the blame game and deflect responsibility. Which are you? Do you need a heart transplant?

3. BE THE TRUTH

The third cornerstone for taking responsibility rather than assigning blame is integrity. Always speak the truth. Jesus said, "I am . . . the truth" (John 14:6). So if you want to lead and live like Christ, integrity is the key. The story has been passed down that a preacher was late leaving his office to attend his little girl's birthday party. His only responsibility for the party was to pick up his daughter's two favorite CDs. Running late, he ran into the store, grabbed the two CDs and one that he wanted, paid for them, and headed to his car. It suddenly dawned on him that those three CDs were really cheap. So he looked at his receipt and noticed that the cashier had only charged him for two CDs. Now he had a decision to make. . . . He went back into the store and shared the cashier's mistake with her while pulling out his wallet. The young cashier looked him in the eyes and said, "I didn't make a mistake. I did that on purpose." She went on to say, "I was a guest at your church last Sunday, and you preached on integrity. I just wanted to see if you live what you preach." When you are committed to living truthfully, taking responsibility is easier.

4. ASSUME THE POSITION

Some folks wake up, look in the mirror, and start singing "How Great Thou Art." Others look into the same mirror and think, *Oooh, that's not good.* However you start your day, consider this truth: "Humble yourselves under the mighty power of God, and at the right time he will lift you up in honor" (1 Peter 5:6 NLT). When your goal is to bring honor to God and not to yourself, then it's relatively easy to take responsibility. When I recognize how small I am compared to God, then I measure myself against Him, not my friends. That makes it easy to determine what I should do with responsibility: own it! I was fifteen years old, attending a youth camp in West Texas, when I first heard this wonderful truth: "Only cowards blow someone else's candle out thinking theirs will now shine brighter." Always blaming someone or something keeps us from attaining health, growth, and honor. Proverbs 29:23 sums it up perfectly: "Pride ends in humiliation, while humility brings honor" (NLT).

My mom was right on target: "Never trust a whiner and never become a whiner. They turn rights into wrongs and wrongs into resentment." Choose to own your life by surrendering it to Christ. When you do so, you'll discover how much simpler it is to *Be the Right Guy, Get a Heart Transplant, Be the Truth,* and *Assume the Position.*

It's Not the End of the Story

JERRY PIPES
Jerry Pipes Productions, Lawrenceville, GA

- Moses murdered an Egyptian in cold blood.
- The beautiful Bathsheba was a powerful temptation—and King David failed to resist.
- Peter denied knowing Jesus . . . three times.

We all face challenges, temptations, and obstacles in life. And from time to time all of us fail to conquer, resist, and overcome. But that's never the end of the story.

- God protected Moses when he fled Egypt, grew him into a man of faith, and used him to lead His people out of captivity.
- David confessed his sin and finished strong. In fact, we know him as a man after God's own heart.
- A few short weeks after betraying his Savior, Peter—forgiven and restored—preached, and on that day of Pentecost more than three thousand people believed and were baptized.

Failure is not the end of the story! Here are some truths that can help you get to your next chapter.

NEED #1: BIG DREAMS

People who win in life have a big dream. When temptation, failure, and setbacks arise, their dream keeps them from quitting. As movie producer and director Cecil B. DeMille put it, "The person who makes a success of living is the one who sees his goal steadily and aims for it unswervingly." Jessica Cox is an example of exactly that:

> Jessica Cox came into this world, a beautiful baby girl, in 1983. Due to a rare birth defect she was born without arms. For some people this obstacle would

be insurmountable. However, Jessica chose to embrace her differences. She abandoned her prosthetic arms by the age of fourteen, deciding that they handicapped her. Jessica's positive attitude and commitment to excellence motivated her to aim for the stars. She took dance lessons, brushed her hair, put on makeup and graduated high school like any other girl. She went on to earn a bachelor's degree in psychology from the University of Arizona. At the age of twenty-five she became the first licensed armless pilot. The airplane has no alterations to accommodate her "disability." Neither does her car, which she is licensed to drive without limitation. Jessica decided early in life to aim BIG. She never quits and she never uses the word *can't*.[1]

Huge dreams kept Jessica Cox from quitting. Let your God-sized dreams keep you moving when you fail.

NEED #2: HARD WORK

Success doesn't come easily—or everyone would be successful! Great achievement requires hard work. As Solomon said, "Hard work always pays off" (Proverbs 14:23 MSG). Thomas Edison agreed: "Genius is 1 percent inspiration and 99 percent perspiration." Asked about his many failures while attempting to invent the lightbulb, he quipped, "I have not failed. I have just found ten thousand ways that won't work." And those ten thousand attempts required painstaking research, long hours, and endless effort. Then came success.

REALIZATION #1: AS ZIG ZIGLAR SAID, "FAILURE IS AN EVENT, NOT A PERSON."

People make wrong choices when they listen to wrong voices—and Satan's voice is a wrong voice. He will say, "You're a failure, a total loser. And you are what you are; you can't change. So cut your losses and just give up!" Don't listen to the enemy. He is a liar and an accuser. Listen instead to God's voice of truth: "You are the righteousness of Christ and more than a conqueror. You are forgiven for your sins: they have been removed as far as the east is from the west. And you can do all things through Christ who strengthens you" (see Romans 2:21–26; 8:37; 1 John 1:9; Psalm 103:12; Philippians 4:13 RSV). Receive God's forgiveness, forgive yourself, learn from the failure, and try again. Follow Paul's advice by "forgetting what lies behind and straining forward to what lies ahead" (3:13 RSV). Satan will try to steal your future by constantly reminding you of your past failures. Jesus, however, has forgiven your past and will never remind you of it again. Instead, He will point you to His plan for the future.

REALIZATION #2: FAILURE IS NEVER FATAL UNLESS YOU LET IT BE FINAL.

We all make mistakes, sin, experience setbacks, and feel intense frustration. As Solomon wrote, "The righteous man falls seven times, and rises again" (Proverbs 24:16 RSV). So keep getting up! Remember, failure is never fatal. Don't quit!

SOOOO . . .

The determining factor between those who accomplish amazing things and those who settle for less is not the absence of failure and difficulty; rather, it's the presence of a big dream and the determination to—by God's grace and in His power—achieve it at any cost.

Set goals: write your dreams on paper—and include a deadline.

Be a lifelong learner: read great books, attend inspirational events, spend time with successful people and learn from them.

Work harder and longer than required: always go the extra mile.

Develop your relationship with Christ: you can't do what He put you here to do without His direction and power.

Thank You, Redeemer God, that—by Your grace—my failures are not the end of the story.

The Quitting Complex

DR. JAY STRACK
Student Leadership University, Orlando, FL

ere's a basic lesson for life: decide right now that whenever you feel like quitting, you simply won't!

Now, I freely admit that, all my life, I've had a great need for an extra helpings of what I call *patient tenacity*. It just doesn't come naturally to me. As a student, I didn't finish most of what I started. I was constantly distracted from my studies, and I fizzled out when things got difficult. I don't like to wait long for anything.

LET PATIENCE DO ITS WORK

One day I talked about this weakness with a godly friend (this kind of relationship is one of my greatest sources of strength for life), and he shared with me a definition of *patient endurance* that transformed my life.

Romans 15:5 says that He is "the God of patience and comfort." *Perseverance* is defined as "not the ability to sit down and bear things, but the ability to rise up and conquer them." Author and commentator William Barclay wrote, "God is He who gives us the power to use any experience to lend greatness and glory to life. God is He in whom we learn to use joy and failure, achievement and disappointment alike, to enrich and to ennoble life, to make us more useful to others and to bring us nearer to Himself"[1]

DIAL DOWN THE STRESS

One of my personal priorities—and the key to my living so I don't quit—is to let God's Word show me where I am wrong, encourage me when I am right, and fuel me daily so that I don't quit. I also know that, first and foremost, I must have my personal roles (listed below) in harmony before I can begin anything new, before I can finish anything I've started, and as I start a day. You may want to work toward that same goal.

* Role #1: You are *a child of the King* and a committed follower of the Lord Jesus Christ. Therefore your life needs to be centered on honoring Him, spending time with Him, and growing in your relationship with Him. And, quite simply, God is to be the first word and the last word in every decision of life.

* Role #2: Healthy *family relationships* are essential to emotional and spiritual health. Give your best—in both word and deed—to parents and siblings. If you aren't willing to work on these relationships, it's doubtful you will do well in any other relationships. (By the way, the Lord knows about your family and understands your thoughts and feelings. My family was a train wreck. Whether or not yours is stable, you must focus on what you can do to fill your role in the family in a healthy way.)

* Role #3: Be *a curious and interested learner* so you can dream dreams, make plans, and reach goals. And master the basics of learning: good study habits, effective time and project management, and thinking both critically and Christianly about decisions.

* Role #4: *Leading others* happens both intentionally and unintentionally as we go through life. But being involved in more leadership roles does not necessarily mean you will impact more people. So choose carefully what you will be involved in. Be thoughtful and in prayer so you keep stress down by not joining or doing too much.

King David thanked the Lord for "[relieving] me in my distress" (Psalm 4:1). The original Hebrew wording pictures an army trapped in a small area and surrounded by the enemy. Similarly, stress captures us and holds us hostage, but God makes room for us to breathe, grow, and even enjoy life when we have our basic roles in life in His—and therefore a healthy—order.

TEN BYTES TO GET TO THE GOAL

Once we have made the commitment to ourselves to endure with patient strength and have prioritized both our time and our emotions regarding our basic roles in life, we can move on to practical steps toward our goal of never quitting:

1. Ask yourself, *Why do I want to quit?* Facing and then understanding your emotions can give insight to make the right choices. Prayer helps too!

2. Examine the work you have already done, and consider whether you should take a new direction or ask for help rather than quitting altogether.

3. Write down all the good things that have happened in your life and title it "My Gratitude List." What insights, wisdom, ideas, or friendships have you gained as a result of undertaking that specific project?

4. Turn weakness into strength. Weaknesses can drive us to depend on God, and that is always a good thing.

5. Evaluate how you spend your time throughout the day. Are you living according to your priorities?

6. Accept responsibility for mistakes you've made. You can blame systems and other people all day long, but that does nothing to get you to your goal.

7. Plan new goals. Look for pieces of the overall plan that you can focus on, complete, and enjoy as small victories along the way.

8. Look at failures as lessons on how to succeed—and never let yesterday take up too much of today.

9. Seek godly counsel.

10. Each week evaluate your progress and make any necessary adjustments to your path toward your goals.

#relationships

It's a Verb

JOHNNY PARKER
The Parker Group, LLC, Spencerville, MD

Yes, you read that right. Okay, if you ask your English teacher, she's right: the actual word *friendship* is a noun. But real friendship takes action, and in that sense *friendship* is a verb. If you want to be a friend—the kind of real friend we all want to have—you need to know that friendship is an investment. Period.

What do you think—or *do* you think—about friendship? Have you given any thought to what it means to be a friend? What makes a true friend? How do you find one? And—maybe more importantly—are you one?

Before we dig into this thing called friendship a little bit, there are a couple of basic things to keep in mind. First of all, don't confuse *acquaintance* and *friend*. You can know many people, but that doesn't mean all of them are friends. Second—as I said a minute ago—friendships require an investment of time and energy.

So, what is a true friend? A true friend is someone who lets you be who you really are on both good days and bad. And a true friend generally makes you feel good about yourself. And, by the way, you show me your friends, and I'll show you your future.

Now let's walk through a friendship checklist:

"REJOICE WITH THOSE WHO REJOICE."

—Romans 12:15

* A true friend celebrates my successes.
* A true friend helps fuel my dreams.

"FAITHFUL ARE THE WOUNDS OF A FRIEND, BUT THE KISSES OF AN ENEMY ARE DECEITFUL."

—Proverbs 27:6

* A true friend is honest with me about my weaknesses.
* A true friend helps me see blind spots in my life.

"BAD COMPANY CORRUPTS GOOD CHARACTER."

—1 Corinthians 15:33 NIV

* A true friend encourages me to make good choices.
* A true friend shares my passion for doing the right thing.

Okay, you need friends in your life, and you have a general sense of what makes a good friend. So, how do you find these people? Jonathan and David can give us some ideas. (They're in the Old Testament. It's a cool story, so check it out.)

Just like us, Jonathan and David were drawn together because they had *shared interests* and a *natural connection* (1 Samuel 18:1–4). In other words, they each had that "there's just something about that guy" sense. It's like that for us too. We find potential friends in the circles we hang out in—band, baseball, dance, debate—because having something in common is a good foundation for a friendship. But more than that, we are drawn to certain people for reasons we can't really put a finger on. Yet we know it when it happens. There's just something we like about certain people, and we're drawn to them.

Now back to this *friendship* is a verb idea. It can't be a one-way street. If you and your friend are hanging out, but it's all give and no get, you need to rethink this because real, true friends make a commitment to each other. We don't sit down and draw up a friendship contract—"I will do X, and in return you will do Y"—but there has to be give on both sides for a friendship to be real. Think about your friends. Do you both work at the friendship, or is it a one-way street? Hmmm . . .

Let's talk about two keys to keeping your friendships strong. (These double as great hints on how to be the kind of friend you'd like to have.)

1. **Do friendship:** Friendship doesn't just happen. You have to work at it. Call, text, do things together.

2. **Bulk up boundaries:** It's not only okay, but it's absolutely necessary to have boundaries with your friends. Think about where your boundaries are and hold to them. Does a friend make plans and then routinely cancel at the last minute? Not okay. Does a friend drive way too fast and make you feel unsafe? Not okay. Boundaries will protect you and your friends from drama and disagreements you could avoid having. But not even the best of friends can read your mind. Be sure you and your friends talk about the boundaries!

> Friendship doesn't just happen. >

TALK THAT MATTERS

Stuff happens in life, and we have to learn to talk about it. Sure, it's much easier to pretend everything is fine and talk about the newest video game instead. Resist the urge to avoid the conversation that matters. It's hard to go there, but you have to do it. Conflict is hard, but learning how to have the hard conversation is important . . . and it's a skill you'll need all your life.

THE SUN SETS

Sometimes you just have to let a friend go. Once again he's betrayed you or violated your trust. Or she's made some life choices that just don't mesh with your moral core. Or maybe it's no action at all on their part, but all give and no get for you. It's good to be a doer and a giver, but genuine friendship is a two-way street. Let your friendship fade into the sunset if it must. Hard, yes, but you and I both know the sun will rise again!

Life is hard, and you need friends around you. So remember: *friendship* is a verb. Think about the kind of friends you want . . . and then be that kind of person to others. You'll be amazed at who God brings into your life to laugh with, to cry with, to be your BFF.

Building on the Right Stuff

JOHNNY PARKER
The Parker Group, LLC, Spencerville, MD

E very July a sandcastle contest is held at Southern California's Imperial Beach. Hours of time are spent erecting truly magnificent sandcastles. Adding to the challenge is the time frame: the makers of the castles must finish by one o'clock so the judges can decide the winner before the tide rolls in and washes away the masterpieces.

Building relationships is like building a house. A solid foundation is required. Your desire to have friends and to connect well with people is absolutely normal. You were made for relationship. But what blueprint for relationships do you follow? And what are the proper materials for building a relationship that will endure?

Jesus modeled two elements essential to strong relationships: He lived with "grace and truth" (John 1:14).

Grace: a relationship is healthy when someone knows you well—faults and all—and loves you anyway. And grace enables the "anyway." Grace is your willingness to forgive people who disappoint you. At the end of the day, all of us are human. Some people will go out of their way to hurt you, and there are just plain mean kids who bully and then act as if nothing is wrong. But the people who love you—Mom, Dad, siblings, grandparents, real friends—don't set out to cause you grief. Your brother did not wake up today and say to himself, "You know, I'm really going to try and hurt my sister today." People who really care about one another want to do the right thing. Really. Yet each of us is a work in progress, so be slow to cast the first stone. That's grace. Grace tempers my expectations of the people who love me. And grace reminds me that I am human just as they are.

Truth: allow God's Word to be the blueprint by which you build your life and relationships. To build according to any other plan is building a sandcastle that will wash away. Keep in mind, though, that building according to God's blueprint doesn't protect you from difficulties in relationships. Your relationships with family members and friends will, at times, get messy. People are imperfect and will fall short of your expectations. So develop the emotional muscles to honestly face and lovingly work through conflict.

With grace and truth as your foundation, you can take the next step toward building rock-solid relationships.

1. **Just do it.** (Yes, I'm borrowing from a famous footwear giant.) And I don't mean it the way you're thinking. All relationships take work: you need to actively build and protect them. Text your sibling who is away at college, invite your mom out to coffee—and put your phone away while you talk to her, give your grandparents a call. It's easy to take these relationships for granted when you live at home, but do practice these skills now. They are absolutely necessary to keeping a relationship alive. *Serve one another* (Galatians 5:13).

2. **Honor.** If you got the latest iPhone or a fancy new car, how would you treat them? I'm guessing with a great deal of care because of how valuable the item is to you. Take this value, multiply it a thousand times, and that is how special you should treat the people who are important to you. Honor is a choice. Practice it today for great results tomorrow. *Honor one another* (Romans 12:10).

3. **Encouragement.** Practice encouragement with and without words . . . a hug, a smile, a high five . . . and put words that make others feel good in your everyday track. Some ideas are:

   * "Thanks. I really appreciate how you . . ."
   * "I believe in you."
   * "It's cool the way you . . ."

Make it a goal to say one encouraging thing to a friend or member of your family every day. "Encourage one another" (1 Thessalonians 5:11 ESV).

In talking about relationships, it would be just plain wrong of me not to talk about sex. I know, you don't really want to go there, but on the other hand, you think about it, wonder about it, and maybe even obsess over it sometimes. So let's go there.

Again, I am going to call out what you see, read, and hear all around you. Just because the shows on television portray high school students having co-ed sleepovers, songs all over the airwaves are about "hooking up," and books galore explain teen sex scenes in rapt detail, this behavior is a *choice*. There is nothing wrong with you for choosing a different path. In fact, as a counselor of thousands of couples facing a marriage crisis, I can almost guarantee you that having sex before you are married will bring you nothing but heartache down the road.

When you have been practicing the relationship skills we've talked about and then meet a person you think is special enough to date exclusively, you are drawn to them, and it's natural for this attraction to make you think about sex . . . a lot. You have to decide long before becoming involved with someone that you aren't going to give in to your body. Don't wait to think this through, because when the moment comes, your mind will be a blur. Your body will fight to take over. If you start having sex, you will spend all your time having sex. Your brain and heart will get confused between true, lifelong love and sex. One day, years later, you will wake up next to this person you realize you don't really know . . . because all those hours you should have been spending really learning about him or her were spent having sex. Don't fall into this trap.

Make the decision for yourself NOW to honor God with your body. Save this important part of yourself for the one person you are going to spend the rest of your life with. It's worth it!

Who Am I?

RON COONEY
Calvary Baptist Church, Clearwater, FL

"He must increase, but I must decrease."

JOHN THE BAPTIST IN JOHN 3:30

Picture yourself in a small room with nine other students. You've been given simple instructions: "Raise your hand when I point to the longest line on the board." The teacher points to the second longest line on the board, and everyone confidently raises a hand—except you. You look around at the hands and then back at the board to make sure you haven't missed anything. You're certain they're wrong, but you reason, "They must know something I don't." So you put your hand up.

This scenario played itself out repeatedly when psychologist Ruth W. Brenda performed an experiment several years ago to see how teenagers would react under peer pressure. Seventy-five percent of the time, the teenagers folded and raised a hand.[1]

But peer pressure isn't an issue just for America's youth. It's one of those things you'll continue to deal with until you're in your nineties. Peer pressure affects every age group—those at the bottom, at the top, and over the hill. It has contributed to scandals like Watergate and such atrocities as the Holocaust. It happens each day on playgrounds, in schools, at businesses, in homes, and, yes, even in churches.

VALUES

Peer pressure isn't so much about the negative influences around you but about the heart within you. That's why, early on in our student ministry, my team defined the six principles we wanted our graduating seniors to know and live by as they entered the real world.

- **Discerning choices:** applying biblical principles to decisions
- **Radicalfaith:** raising the risk for Jesus on a daily basis
- **Include others:** putting others first
- **Valuable relationships:** having intentional relationships with others
- **Entrusted authority:** honoring the authority God has established
- **Noble boundaries:** setting boundaries in friendships

As my team established what would become the bedrock of our student ministry, two verses set the tone for how those values would be lived out:

> If anyone desires to come after Me, let him deny himself, and take up his cross daily, and follow Me. For whoever desires to save his life will lose it, but whoever loses his life for My sake will save it. (Jesus in Luke 9:23–24)

> He must increase, but I must decrease. (John the Baptist in John 3:30)

When you put your faith in Jesus, you aren't just calling Him "Savior" in order to escape hell; you're also calling Him "Lord" because He is the One who sets the standards for how you live your life. The Bible becomes your how-to manual and the Holy Spirit your Guide. And this begins the process of denying yourself—Jesus becomes more and you become less. As this happens, the problem of peer pressure begins to take care of itself. But it *is* a process.

WHO AM I?

So who exactly are you in Christ? You are "a new creation" (2 Corinthians 5:17). You are "a chosen race, a royal priesthood . . . a people for his own possession" (1 Peter 2:9 ESV). Your body is a "temple of the Holy Spirit" (1 Corinthians 6:19). You are "His workmanship, created in Christ Jesus for good works" (Ephesians 2:10). You are a child of God (John 1:12), and your "citizenship is in heaven" (Philippians 3:20). You are "the body of Christ" (1 Corinthians 12:27). You are the branches and Jesus is the Vine (John 15:5).

Are you starting to get the picture? You are not your own, so of course you operate by a different set of rules than the world offers. No wonder those who refuse to put themselves under the authority of Christ are going to be different. They will act, talk, and think differently. Not only that, but the Bible clearly states that there will be more people who create their own rules to live by than those who honor God (Matthew 7:13–14)—and that means plenty of pressure from all sides.

BOUNDARIES

Land has property lines. Sports have out-of-bounds. Games have rules. If you share a room, I'll bet even your room has a line drawn to show whose turf is whose. The same should be true with your friendships. Every healthy relationship has boundaries. It's a way to communicate that we love someone.

And boundaries go back to the garden of Eden. God considered all that He had made good, and then He set a boundary: Adam was not to eat the fruit of a particular tree (Genesis 2:15–17). Every good parent sets boundaries, or rules, around their children just as God did for Adam and Eve. Boundaries keep children safe and communicate love. You would be wise to follow God's example and your parents': set boundaries in your friendships.

Now, your friends likely won't understand. Be ready for their resistance when you say no to alcohol or drugs. For backup, let your parents be your scapegoat. Have a private conversation with your folks, and let them know that you don't want to give in to peer pressure, so you'd like to use them as an excuse for not doing whatever the crowd might want you to do if you are uncomfortable or know what they are doing is wrong. If your mom or dad won't be that person for you, remember that you have a heavenly Father who will.

The point of not giving in to peer pressure is to learn early on how to bring God glory in every area of your life. If you put your faith in Jesus, develop a framework upon which to build your life, and set boundaries with your friends, you put yourself in a position where God can bless and use you for His purposes.

Iron Sharpening Iron

MIKE CALHOUN
Word of Life Fellowship, Schroon Lake, NY

ccountability is one of those words that is frequently used but often misunderstood. In Christian circles, the word causes many people to bristle. Maybe because of a bad experience with an overzealous discipler. Maybe because we like our independence. Accountability, however, is one of the keys to the successful Christian life.

Consider these aspects of accountability:

Measurement: To be held accountable is to be measured, graded, or evaluated. Nobody enjoys being graded, but the wise understand its importance. You are changing and growing all the time, often faster than you realize. Measurement is important if you care about how you are changing and into what kind of person you are becoming.

Responsibility: God will hold each one of us responsible for our own choices (Romans 14:10–12). Being accountable to another person until then serves as a more immediate and tangible reminder of that fact.

Limitation of power: Adolescence is a time of growing independence and increasing freedom, but—and this is true throughout life, whatever our age— our freedom to choose must be curbed by a higher authority. Accountability simply means that each one of us must answer to someone.

YOUR BRAIN

And science tells us that students need accountability more urgently than anyone else on earth, and basic physiology is an important reason why. The teenage mind is a fascinating thing. For starters, it more easily makes connections between neurons than a fully developed adult brain does. Put simply, you have a high capacity for learning[1] and you are highly susceptible to addiction.[2]

And did you know that the last piece of a student's brain to develop is the prefrontal lobe, where risk is measured?[3]

Think about the biology of what is happening to you. Your mind is able to process huge amounts of information very quickly, you are experiencing many things for the very first time, and the part of your brain that measures risk is underdeveloped. Do you understand now why your parents are just hoping you survive to see twenty-five?

> Accountability is a tool that can help you live up to your own ambitions. >

ACCOUNTABILITY THAT WON'T CRUSH A SOUL

Most students like you have high expectations for themselves. Accountability is a tool that can help you live up to your own ambitions. Like any tool, though, accountability can be misused. It can too easily become a bludgeon used to force compliance to a religious standard. What kind of accountability system will enrich a life rather than crush a soul? I'm glad you asked. Here's what you can offer—and therefore what you would be wise to look for—in an accountability relationship.

1. SEEK FIRST TO UNDERSTAND

Ask lots of questions. Don't assume that you know what is happening inside a friend's mind and heart. Use "why" and "how" questions to lead your friends to a clear and specific articulation of their spiritual goals: "Study my Bible for twenty minutes every morning." When your friends have set a personal goal like this, you will be able to ask about their progress and gently remind them when they fall short of the standard they set for themselves.

2. BE A COACH, NOT A COP

You know the difference, right? A cop enforces a standard that has been imposed on you from the outside. A coach helps you strategize and develop the ability to reach your own goals, the ones you set for yourself. It is very important that every individual set his or her own spiritual goals.

3. FIND PEER-LEVEL ACCOUNTABILITY

Adolescence is the time to "put away childish things" (1 Corinthians 13:11 KJV). One of the best ways to do this is to be accountable to someone other than your parents. Of course you ought to honor your parents, but you also need to become spiritually independent. So seek out other believers to hold you accountable. Choosing your own accountability partner is a great way to gain some independence without becoming isolated from the greater community of the church.

The science of brain development suggests that being accountable to someone is a good idea. So does the challenge to live in a way that honors God when our immoral culture throws temptations our way 24/7. And the pressures of trying to keep the faith in our post-modern twenty-first-century world suggest that it's not wise to go it alone. So find someone (of the same sex) who will hold you accountable to living the way God wants you to live—and hold that person accountable as well. Be for each other iron sharpening iron.

Are Girls Really That Different from Guys?

CANDI FINCH
Southwestern Theological Seminary, Fort Worth, TX

I n today's society, there is a trend toward making things—everything from bathrooms to the language we use to college dorm rooms—gender neutral. This trend can subtly influence our thinking and prompt us to wonder, "Is there anything other than the obvious biological differences that makes girls distinct from guys?" Many people aren't sure how to answer this question.

One reason for this confusion is the message our culture sends young women. The woman who takes control of her sexuality and uses it to get what she wants is celebrated and seen as empowered. Turn on a movie or TV show aimed at teens: a young woman who chooses a Christian approach to life is often ridiculed and seen as backward, sending the not-so-subtle message to young Christian women that doing things God's way is not realistic or respectable in our modern society.

No wonder the Bible warns us believers about becoming so well-adjusted to the culture that we start fitting in without even thinking about it (Romans 12:2). We must be careful that we aren't accepting the world's message about what it means to be a woman over what God teaches us about our identity.

THE PURPOSE OF OUR CREATION

God created men and women as distinct, yet complementary beings (Genesis 1:27; 2:18). While both girls and guys are created in the image of God (Genesis 1:27), God had a specific purpose in mind when He created Eve: she was to be a "helper" for Adam (Genesis 2:18, 20). But being a helper does not imply that Eve was inferior to Adam in any way. It simply reveals God's plan for cooperation rather than competition in a marriage. Men and women need each other, and that important truth about community has been part of God's plan from the beginning (Genesis 2:18).

THE SIGNIFICANCE OF DISTINCTIONS

So what does it look like for a woman to be a helper? When a marriage relationship is described in the Bible, the wife is called to submit to and respect her husband as unto the Lord and at the same time the husband is called to love his wife just as Christ loved the church (Ephesians 5:22–33; Colossians 3:18–19). Why would God ask this of wives? Because the way a husband and wife interact with each other should be a picture of the way God interacts with the church (Ephesians 5:32). Christian marriages are to be witnesses to lost people about the way Christ (pictured in husbands) loves the church (pictured in wives). Our sexuality is not about us; it was designed to reveal the heart and character of God.

WHY DOES GOD'S PLAN MATTER?

The thought patterns, actions, and habits you cultivate today often determine the path you will take tomorrow. So how should an understanding of God's plan impact young women on a daily basis, especially if a trip down the altar isn't imminent? Here are three ways that a right understanding of God's plan for women will impact you on a daily basis:

1. How you view yourself. What the world says about an "ideal" woman changes. During the Renaissance, for instance, the standard of beauty was a very pale woman who was not skinny because those two traits meant that she didn't work outside and that her family was wealthy enough that she had plenty to eat. In sharp contrast, today's models are often underweight. So cultural values change, but God's ideals never change. He says that we are His work of art (Ephesians 2:10), that He formed us exactly as He wanted us (Psalm 139:13–14), and that what is on the inside is more important than what is on the outside

(1 Samuel 16:7; 1 Peter 3:3–4; Proverbs 31:30). How you view yourself will be determined by where you look. Are you looking to Christ or to culture to form your opinions about yourself and what it means to be a young woman?

2. How you treat guys. Knowing that God's plan is for girls and guys to cooperate, not compete, will impact how you treat guys. A foolish woman views guys as prey and seeks to control them through her words and sexuality. She uses her words to flatter and entice guys (Proverbs 2:16; 5:3; 6:24; 7:21; 22:14), and she tempts them to sin (Proverbs 2:18–19; 23:27–28). God desires that His children be "blameless and pure" in the midst of a crooked and depraved generation (Philippians 2:15 NIV), but the sad truth is that our modern culture encourages girls to be provocative and enticing. You can nevertheless enjoy healthy interactions with your guy friends, encouraging one another toward godliness rather than being a stumbling block for each other (Hebrews 3:13; Romans 14:13).

3. What kind of guys you date. You should only date guys you respect and would be willing to submit to if you were married. Is the guy pressuring you into a physical relationship? He is not worthy of your respect. Does he encourage you to become closer to God? Then he may be a keeper! The Bible is clear that you should not date someone who is an unbeliever (2 Corinthians 6:14), but you should also not date someone who cannot be a spiritual leader. One of the guys you date will eventually become your husband, so don't compromise your values as you make decisions about dating. Remember, God's plan is for a Christian husband and wife to be a bright witness for the gospel!

History is full of young women who have committed to follow God's unique plan for their lives, and their examples still speak to us today. Read about biblical women like Ruth (Ruth 1–4), Esther (Esther 1–10), and Mary (Luke 1), or get to know women in church history like Ann Judson (1789–1826), Amy Carmichael (1867–1951), or Manche Masemola (1911–1928).

Girls are different from guys—and that's God's plan!

Guarding Your Heart

STEVE BROWNING
Hebron Baptist Church, Dacula, GA

What's on your checklist?

Admit it. Most people have one in their mind, if not written down. I'm talking about the list of traits that you would like to find in the perfect dateable person. Your list might include personality traits: *has a good sense of humor* or *is mature*. You may have specifics about appearance: *5'4"* or *6'2"*; *auburn hair* or *definitely a blonde*. Perhaps you even mention certain abilities: *athletic* or *intelligent*. Whatever is on your list (and you know you have one), you probably have an idea of what you are looking for in that special someone you want to date. But what about the things God wants to see in the person you date?

Literally hundreds of books on the subject of dating have been written from a Christian perspective. (Or is it courting?) We can, however, glean some important and essential principles straight from the greatest Christian text of all: the Bible. While the Bible is hardly a dating guide, it does talk about relationships between a man and a woman. It may not lay out the specific person you are supposed to date: " 'Bobby, thou shalt asketh out Susie, for she is of fine appearance, and I will surely bless your request.' And Bobby rejoiced greatly." But God does have some specific requirements that should be on your checklist.

We'll look at three of God's requirements, starting with the most important. If someone doesn't meet Priority #1, don't bother looking for Priority #2. If any of these priorities is not met, then this person isn't the best dating choice after all.

PRIORITY #1: IS THIS PERSON A CHRISTIAN?

Second Corinthians 6:14 says, "Do not be unequally yoked together with unbelievers. For what fellowship has righteousness with lawlessness? And what communion has light with darkness?" This verse encourages us to make sure that we form our closest friendships with believers. If this principle is true for your friendships, how much more should it apply to your dating relationships! "Being yoked" to someone means being attached to that person. If the person goes to the right, you go to the right. If that person goes to the left, you go to the left. The point is that people we are close to tend to influence the direction we go. For this reason, one of the priorities we find in Scripture is that we are to date only Christians.

PRIORITY #2: DOES THIS PERSON ENCOURAGE ME TO GROW IN MY FAITH?

In writing to husbands and wives, the author of Ephesians charged husbands to "love your wives, just as Christ also loved the church and gave Himself for her, that He might sanctify and cleanse her with the washing of water by the word" (5:25–26). The idea here is that, in a Christian relationship, each person is to encourage the other to embrace

> In a Christian relationship, each person is to encourage the other to embrace God's Word and live by His standards and His principles. **>**

God's Word and live by His standards and His principles. Put simply, if you are dating someone who is encouraging you to live contrary to God's Word, then you are in a bad relationship, and that means it may be time to reassess your Facebook status. The person you date should encourage you in your walk with Christ rather than hinder it.

PRIORITY #3: HAVE YOU AND THE OTHER PERSON PRAYED ABOUT BEING IN THIS RELATIONSHIP?

Ephesians 5:21 talks about believers "submitting to one another out of reverence for Christ" (ESV). The reason we enter into a dating relationship with another person should be because we believe God is leading us into that relationship. But—and this is key—don't ignore the first two priorities and think that God is leading you into a relationship that doesn't meet those standards.

> The person you date should encourage you in your walk with Christ rather than hinder it. >

This would be contrary to God's instruction in Scripture, and God will never lead us to disobey His Word. So pray before entering a dating relationship. Do your best to discern God's will.

Does following these three priorities mean you will never have your heart broken again? Are they a magical formula for finding "the one"? Probably not, but they can certainly save you a lot of heartache by guarding you from relationships you should not have entered in the first place. So put these three priorities at the top of your list and then invite God to edit other items you've included according to His priorities and His great love for you.

Challenging, but Not Impossible

DENNIS STEEGER
Grace Outreach, Plano, TX

O nce upon a time . . . little girls dreamed of Prince Charming winning their heart. Little boys dreamed of heroically saving the kingdom from danger. Together they dreamed of the fairy-tale marriage, described perfectly as *happily ever after.*

Today those grown-up children are finding their childhood dreams shattered. For too many couples, marriage isn't the fairy-tale life together they had hoped for. Instead, their life together is a heartbreaking tragedy. The latest statistics tell us that approximately 50 percent of married couples today will divorce. Families—the primary relational unit God has established—will be destroyed. What was to be a lifetime of love and faithfulness will instead be years of disillusionment and heartbreak.

Not insignificantly—and no wonder—many students find the notion of being with one person "till death do us part" a very unlikely proposition. Staying married is definitely challenging, but it is important to note that the process is challenging, *not* impossible. Got that? Challenging, *not* impossible.

Also, it's difficult to overstate the importance of staying married. Statistical data reveals that married couples are happier, more successful, and healthier than people who are single or who have remarried. Children do much better relationally, academically, and even financially when their biological parents stay together. In fact, divorce is one of the leading predictors of poverty for women. Our country and our communities are stronger and safer when families stay together. It is absolutely vital for the good of our society that we learn how to stay married. It is imperative that, once we get married, we stay married.

I believe the reason many marriages fail is because many people who are getting married are not prepared to *be* married. We prepare for months to have an awesome *wedding*, but we do very little preparation for an awesome *marriage*. Preparation for life after the wedding is infinitely more important than planning for any aspect of the wedding—and preparation for marriage starts now! Now is the time for you to work on *becoming* the right person you need to be to stay married, not on *finding* the right person.

No one gets married with plans to divorce; no one makes vows they intend to break. Many of those who say, "I do" simply haven't developed the character necessary for keeping those most important promises they will ever make. It's not that any of us are bad people; we are just people who do not possess a well-developed character. We don't want to be bad, but we lack the capacity to be good more consistently. Marriages fail because we lack the moral strength to keep our promises and remain faithful to each other.

Character deficiency is not something sparked by getting married; character deficiency is a lifetime in the making. As children, for instance, we realized that lying was better than telling the truth because it protected us from the consequences of our actions. We learned that blaming other people is better than taking responsibility for our actions because it alleviates any feelings of guilt or failure. When character is not forged in the fires of personal responsibility, the results are weakness in our resolve and an inability to follow through on our commitments.

So how do we prepare ourselves for marriage? You know what I'm going to say: I believe we must develop our character. A well-developed character is the super glue of relationships. A well-developed character enables trust, that stickiness factor that too many relationships lack. As you may have realized, trust is difficult to earn and easy to lose, so we must do everything possible to develop our character.

Key to the development of character is our purity, both physical and mental. I believe that sexual purity is a huge factor in determining our capacity for long-term faithfulness. In fact, sexual activity before marriage is a leading predictor of future divorce. It's not because sexual sin is worse than other sins; it's just that sexual sin carries a different set of consequences. One consequence of sexual sin is that it weakens our ability to be faithful. Another consequence of sexual sin is that it destroys trust. The ability to remain faithful and trustworthy is the foundation on which a marriage is built.

Our ability to cultivate trusting relationships is crucial. In a world where commitment to a person is only an inch deep, our relational shallowness leads to a belief that all relationships are disposable. For instance, when a son experiences the departure and desertion of his father, he develops a sense of independence. The son begins to think to himself, *I don't need anyone but me.* While that may sound good at first glance, the Bible tells us to trust in the Lord (Proverbs 3:5). God wants us to depend on Him primarily and to depend on a spouse in a partnership for life.

Our character also develops as we learn to keep our word. As James put it so straightforwardly, "Let your 'Yes' be 'Yes,' and your 'No,' 'No'" (James 5:12). Keeping our promises to others increases both the trust and respect needed to sustain lasting relationships.

Furthermore, a well-developed character enables us to keep people's trust once we earn it. And a well-developed character is evident when you keep your promises, do what you say you will do, show up on time, call your girlfriend when you say you will, obey your curfew, honor your commitments, tell the truth, and take responsibility for your actions and decisions.

Staying married takes a lot of work—and that work starts now. You will never have more time to develop your character for marriage than you do right now—yet you will probably never be less motivated to prepare your character than you are right now. But know that developing character and character-preserving habits will help you sustain a "till death do us part" relationship.

Seven Cs for Dealing with Conflict

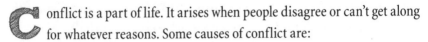
RICK YOUNG
First Baptist Church, Woodstock, GA

Conflict is a part of life. It arises when people disagree or can't get along for whatever reasons. Some causes of conflict are:

* Having different views on an issue
* Having different goals
* Not understanding another person
* Simply not getting along

The list goes on, but these are just symptoms. The root of the issue? James asked the same question and then answered it:

> What causes quarrels and what causes fights among you? Is it not this, that your passions are at war within you? You desire and do not have, so you murder. You covet and cannot obtain, so you fight and quarrel. You do not have, because you do not ask. You ask and do not receive, because you ask wrongly, to spend it on your passions. (James 4:1–3 ESV)

Conflict starts in the heart, a truth that Jesus had acknowledged earlier: "Out of the heart come evil thoughts, murder, adultery, sexual immorality, theft, false witness, slander" (Matthew 15:19 ESV). According to the book of Proverbs, the heart is the wellspring of life, so we must protect what enters it, and we must pay attention to both what comes out of it and what it reveals to us about ourselves. Conflict, for instance, can bring out the worst in all of us—but it doesn't have to. In fact, conflict doesn't have to be a bad thing; it can be something that, if handled correctly, strengthens us and our relationships.

This is where the Seven Cs come into play. These seven steps can help us deal with conflict in a way that honors God.

Call on God. When experiencing conflict, seek wisdom from God. Whatever the situation, He will give you clear direction on how to proceed. God is interested in your life, in your problems, and in your heart, and He wants you to call on Him for wisdom. Why? So you can bring honor to His name as you learn how to get along better with others in your life.

Check your emotions. As a human being dealing with conflict, you may get very emotional in the moment, and your emotions can interfere with how well you handle conflict. So try to look at a situation without letting how you feel determine how you will act. That doesn't mean you can't tell someone how you feel. Just don't let your emotions be the only factor or the key factor that determines your behavior.

Consider the other person's point of view. Often when we are dealing with a conflict of some kind, we look only at what we think is right. When dealing with friends or family members, however, it is good to look at the situation from their perspective. This different point of view may help you see something important that you have missed, and you may recognize they have a valid point.

Communicate in person. A conflict is never handled the right way when we don't address the issue face-to-face. Technology is a great tool. Phone calls, texts, e-mail, Facebook, and Twitter are great ways to keep in touch with people, but they are not the best ways to deal with conflict. The person with whom you're trying to resolve a conflict needs to be able to hear not only your point of view but also the emotions behind the words. Person to person is still the best way to resolve a conflict.

Confront in love. When you go to the person with whom you have a conflict, always go in love. We see in the Bible that God deals with us in His lovingkindness (Psalm 36:10; 40:11; 42:8). Going in love will always start the process off right. This godly approach will help you resolve the conflict.

Careful with your words. As Proverbs 15:1 says, "A soft answer turns away wrath, but a harsh word stirs up anger." How you say things—the words and tone of voice and the facial expressions you choose—can help or hinder your efforts to resolve a conflict. Calmly speaking words that lead to fixing the problem will always help. When you make comments that hurt or that you don't really mean, the conflict can get much worse very quickly. Thoughtless comments will prolong the healing process and can even ruin a relationship. The words you choose as well as the way you choose to say them do matter, so choose wisely.

Create peace. Jesus taught, "Blessed are the peacemakers, for they shall be called sons of God" (Matthew 5:9). Peacemakers are those who show grace to others even during hard times. God calls us to create peace in any and every conflict we deal with. Sometimes efforts to resolve a conflict can start off rough, but the goal is to make peace and as a result enjoy a healthier, stronger relationship.

Conflict can enslave you, keep you focused on yourself, and destroy your relationships. And Satan—the "thief" who comes "to steal, and to kill, and to destroy"—would love for that to happen (John 10:10). Wanting to ruin your life and the lives of your friends and family, your enemy will interfere with your efforts to resolve a conflict, but God has a different plan.

God wants you to experience freedom; God does not want you to be a slave of conflicts. He wants every conflict in your life to be resolved in ways that make your relationships grow stronger. It's not easy, but dealing with a conflict can help you grow. If you just ignore conflicts, however, you won't benefit in any way. Face your conflicts and watch God work.

> In the middle of difficulty lies opportunity.
>
> > —Albert Einstein

Don't Mess with Poison

JOHN LEATHERS
First Baptist North Spartanburg, Spartanburg, SC

God created us to be in relationship. When He looked down on the solitary Adam, He created Eve, another human who enabled Adam to be in relationship with a human being as well as with his Creator, relationships Adam was designed for. Acting on our God-given desire for relationships, we gravitate toward people who have similar interests or who will accept us for who we are. Ideally our search for relationships will lead us to healthy ones. However, for many of us, the need for friendship is so great that we are content with any relationship, even if that relationship is toxic.

What is a toxic relationship? *Toxic* is defined in the *New Oxford Dictionary* as something "very bad, unpleasant, or harmful." In the same dictionary, *relationship* is defined as "the way in which two or more people are connected." Thus, a toxic relationship is a very bad, unpleasant, or harmful connection between two or more people. And that's a relationship you want to run after, right? No! This is the last thing you should be looking for in a relationship, but because of our great and very human need for acceptance, we will sometimes take anything we can get, no matter how harmful or degrading the other person's behavior is. The first question we want to answer is, "How do I even know if I am in a toxic relationship?" For an answer to this question, we are going to go to turn to Scripture, specifically 3 John 1:9–10. These verses do an amazing job describing a toxic relationship:

> I have written something to the church, but Diotrephes, who likes to put himself first, does not acknowledge our authority. So if I come, I will bring up what his is doing, talking wicked nonsense against us. And not content with that, he refuses to welcome the brothers, and also stops those who want to and puts them out of the church. (ESV)

First, a toxic relationship is always *centered on the needs and wants of the other person*. In this passage we see that Diotrephes is only concerned about himself. If you are in a relationship, whether it is a friendship or a dating relationship, and everything seems to be focused on what the other person wants or needs, then you are in a toxic relationship. If you are never given an opportunity to make decisions or if that person is never concerned about your needs, then you are in a toxic relationship. Sometimes it's hard to see when you are in such a relationship, but if all your other friends and the people you trust are telling you that this particular relationship is completely one-sided, then you are in a toxic relationship.

The second characteristic of a toxic relationship is *how the person treats you*. As you read this passage, hopefully you can see what a terrible friend Diotrephes is. Not only is he completely selfish, but he is just flat-out not nice. If you find yourself in a relationship where you are the one constantly being made fun of or always the brunt of the jokes, then you are in a toxic relationship. If you are constantly being put down and made to feel like a worthless person, then you are in a toxic relationship.

> A toxic relationship is always centered on the needs and wants of the other person. **>**

Third, in a toxic relationship, the person *will not like your friends*. Maybe you have befriended a group of people or even finally started dating that person you have had your eye on for months. When you mention to your toxic friend that you want them to meet each other, that toxic friend says something to the effect of, "There is something I've been wanting to tell you. Your friends are idiots, and if you want to hang out with me or date me, then you need to lose those freaks." If you have had this conversation or something similar, then you are in a toxic relationship! If the person you are in a relationship with is selfish and mean and despises your friends, then there is a good chance that you are in an unhealthy relationship and you need to get out.

Scripture tells us that "bad company ruins good morals" (1 Corinthians 15:33 ESV), and if you continue reading the passage we just looked at, it tells us to not imitate what is evil but "imitate . . . what is good" (3 John 1:11). A toxic relationship is called *toxic* for a reason, and it won't ruin just one relationship; it will ruin others as well. You must end this toxic relationship immediately. The best way to end the relationship is to go to that person and say, in love, that this relationship is not working out for you and then cut all ties with that person. If you are in a toxic dating relationship, don't say, "We can't be together, but we can still be friends." This will not work, and the relationship will only get progressively worse. Remember, a toxin is a poison—and you don't mess around with poison.

Yes, I know it's hard to identify a toxic relationship, and it's even more difficult to admit that you are in one. You must be willing to examine the relationships in your life to see if any are toxic. If you identify an unhealthy relationship, then, in a God-honoring way, begin to take the steps you need to take to find your way out.

One more thing—and this is important. In addition to examining the relationships you are in, you must also be willing to examine yourself to make sure you are not the Diotrephes of the relationship. As followers of Christ we are called to be holy or set apart, different from the world, and that means our relationships should be set apart as well. Make sure you are in relationships that are pleasing to your heavenly Father.

Made in God's Image

DEREK SIMPSON
First Baptist Church Cleveland, Cleveland, TN

A doorway had been cut through the lower part of a fifteen-by-twenty-eight-foot painting on one wall of the Santa Maria delle Grazie Church in Milan, Italy. The painting was largely unrecognizable after 150 years of neglect. After many botched attempts, restoration efforts were halted in 1796, and Napoleon's troops used the room as a makeshift prison. A once beautiful piece of art was a canvas for the prisoners' graffiti.

Surprisingly, this unfortunate series of events offers hope for a contemporary and much darker tragedy. Stay with me.

- It is estimated that up to 160,000 students stay home from school each day because they fear being bullied.
- Most research shows that up to 25 percent of all middle- and high school students in the United States are bullied at some point in their teenage years.

Too many young people—God's created masterpieces who bear the image of God (Genesis 1:27)—feel no value, no worth, no purpose.

The truth is that no animal or angel—however beautiful and majestic—compares to a human being. Humans stand alone as the crowning achievement of God's creative work, a reflection of many of His attributes. That's why bullying is so wrong—those God created rebel against the Creator by destroying His precious creations. And bullying goes back to the beginning . . .

Adam and Eve had two boys: Abel, who gained the Lord's favor, and Cain, who merely went through the motions of worship (Genesis 4:1–5). Yet God graciously pursued Cain, offering him a path to reconciliation. Refusing God's invitation, an enraged Cain murdered his brother, Abel.

What does the story of Cain and Abel have to do with bullying today? Everything. After all, bullying occurs when one or more persons repeatedly threaten or harm someone who feels helpless to respond. It can take place in a classroom, lunchroom, office, team, or family. Bullying doesn't always involve physical violence, but it is always terrifying evidence of sin and pride.

Every person who has ever been bullied—as Abel was—is created in the image of God. The divine image is imprinted on even the most socially awkward or annoying person, and that person is supremely valuable, deserving of love and respect.

Every bully is guilty of attacking, if not destroying, a person created in the image of God. Whether driven by jealousy, pride, anger, or simple disdain for their neighbor, bullies are rebelling against the Creator. Jesus indicated the seriousness of bullying when He taught that the Old Testament prohibition of murder is actually a prohibition against anger, a prohibition against bullying: "If you are even angry with someone, you are subject to judgment! If you call someone an idiot, you are in danger of being brought before the court. And if you curse someone, you are in danger of the fires of hell" (Matthew 5:22 NLT).

The neglected painting with a doorway cut into it is Leonardo DaVinci's *The Last Supper.* It survived more failed restoration attempts and World War II bombing before a team of researchers, scientists, and artists began a twenty-one-year restoration project in 1978.

What a great illustration of the work Jesus does in our lives! A once devalued masterpiece is appreciated again in all its stunning beauty. You are that masterpiece.

If you are guilty of bullying, repent of your sin, and seek forgiveness from God and anyone you've hurt. If you have been bullied, ask God to help you both forgive those who have hurt you and trust the Spirit to heal that hurt. God can help you, a once devalued masterpiece, to see the stunning beauty He created. And we are all called to defend those who can't defend themselves and to do everything in our power to ensure that no student is marginalized, criticized, or bullied.

The Myth of Sticks and Stones

SHAUN BLAKENEY
Christ Fellowship, Palm Beach Gardens, FL

People have said, "Sticks and stones will break my bones, but words will never hurt me." That couldn't be further from the truth. Whoever came up with this saying must have been a cold, unfeeling robot! Bones will mend, but words cut the heart and eat at the soul, sometimes for life.

Yet bullying has long been a fact of life. Youth have been bullying one another for years, but your generation of young adults is taking harassment to the next level. With technology reaching new heights every day, students can expand their bullying to harm more people. This vicious phenomenon is called *cyberbullying* and has been defined as "willful and repeated harm inflicted through the use of computers, cell phones, and other electronic devices."[1] Cyberbullying is when young adults use technology, usually cell phones or computers, to embarrass or hassle their peers.

Statics say that more than 30 percent of youth have been the target of cyberbullying. Bullying is prevalent online via e-mail, but it also happens through texting and social networking. And since social networks such as Facebook and Twitter form such an important part of many young adults' social life, victims sometimes feel utterly embarrassed, very exposed, and therefore powerless to do anything about it.

Proverbs 6:16–19 says this: "These six things the LORD hates, yes, seven are an abomination to Him: a proud look, a lying tongue, hands that shed innocent blood, a heart that devises wicked plans, feet that are swift in running to evil, a false witness who speaks lies, and one who sows discord among brethren."

Based on those Proverbs 6 verses, the statement that God hates bullying is not at all a stretch. Scripture is clear that God hates "a lying tongue" and a heart that plots evil. God hates bullying because it tears down the truth about yourself and your value that He has spoken to you. God created you in His image, and He loves

> God hates bullying because it tears down the truth about yourself and your value that He has spoken to you. **>**

all of His children—you included—unconditionally. Satan, however, wants to do everything in his power to sow insecurity and embarrassment into your heart, and generating conflict between people is one method he uses.

And that's why 1 Peter 5:8–10 offers this warning:

> Stay alert! Watch out for your great enemy, the devil. He prowls around like a roaring lion, looking for someone to devour. Stand firm against him, and be strong in your faith. Remember that your Christian brothers and sisters all over the world are going through the same kind of suffering you are. In his kindness God called you to share in his eternal glory by means of Christ Jesus. So after you have suffered a little while, he will restore, support, and strengthen you, and he will place you on a firm foundation. (NLT)

Adolescence is a crucial time of emotional, physical, mental, and spiritual development, so Satan vigorously attacks vulnerable young people like you who are looking for a strong foundation of truth about who you are, truth that gives you a solid sense of value. At this stage of a person's life—when self-confidence is being established and technology is most popular—cyberbullying can leave young adults feeling depressed, angry, unwanted, hopeless, and very much alone.

Again, bullying isn't new, but cyberbullying has taken harassment and hostile words to a new level of intensity and impact. Look back, though, at one story about bullying from the Bible, that battle of words between David and

Goliath. This Philistine bully was a great warrior who thought he couldn't lose a battle, especially to a teenager. What Goliath didn't know was that David had God on his side and that God was all David needed. It was God who gave David and the Israelites the victory that day by guiding one deadly stone to hit Goliath. Don't ever underestimate your power and ability when God is on your side.

And how does that truth apply in the twenty-first century? Here are a couple ways you can help end cyberbullying.

* Be a source of encouragement to those who are being bullied. You can do this by joining their online social networks. In addition to seeing what is being said and who is saying it, engage in chats when you're online. Speak truth when it needs to be spoken and confront with love when that is necessary. After all, the tongue has the power to bring life or bring death (see James 3:2–6).

* Pray. There is real power in prayer because in prayer we are talking directly to the almighty God. So pray every day and ask God to go before you in every situation. Pray and ask Him to give you wisdom so you know how to handle each cyber situation and cyber problem. Pray that if you see someone being bullied, the Lord will give you words of truth that will bring healing and hope.

Remember, God is big. He is the very same God who spoke the world into existence. He is the same God who created mankind from the dust of the earth. And He's the same God who helped David conquer Goliath. He can handle absolutely any bully.

#sex

What Does the Bible Really Say About Sex?

DR. DANNY AKIN
Southeastern Theological Seminary, Wake Forest, NC

In her article "What They Didn't Teach You About Sex in Sunday School," Peggy Fletcher Stack wrote, "Many people assume the Bible has just one message about sex: Don't do it."[1] Well, anyone who says that has obviously not read the Bible. God actually has a lot to say about sex. In fact, sex is a good gift from a great God, and it provides incredible blessings and delights . . . when done God's way!

Sex is—according to God's design—good, exciting, intoxicating, powerful, and unifying. Although the Bible is not a book on sex, it does contain a complete theology of sexuality: the purposes for sex, warnings against its misuse, and a beautiful picture of ideal physical intimacy as set forth in the Song of Solomon. The one-flesh relationship (Genesis 2:24) is the most intense physical intimacy and the deepest spiritual unity possible between a husband and wife. It is exceeded only by our intimacy with the Lord Jesus. God always approves of sex in the context of heterosexual marriage where a husband and wife meet each other's physical needs in sexual intercourse (Proverbs 5:15–21). Both a husband and a wife have definite and equal sexual needs that God says should be met in marriage (1 Corinthians 7:3), and each is to be more concerned about meeting the other's needs than having their own met (Philippians 2:3–5).

God gave us the good gift of sex for several important reasons. These purposes include: (1) intimate oneness (Genesis 2:24); (2) comfort (Genesis 24:67); (3) the creation of life (Genesis 1:28); (4) play and pleasure (Song of Solomon 2:8–17; 4:1–16); and (5) avoiding temptation (1 Corinthians 7:2–5).

In fact, a man is commanded to find satisfaction (Proverbs 5:19) and joy

(Ecclesiastes 9:9) in his wife and to concern himself with meeting her unique needs (Deuteronomy 24:5; 1 Peter 3:7). And a wife has responsibilities to her husband. These include: (1) availability (1 Corinthians 7:3–5); (2) preparation and planning (Song of Solomon 4:9); (3) interest (Song of Solomon 4:16; 5:2); and (4) sensitivity to unique masculine needs (Genesis 24:67). The feeling of oneness experienced by husband and wife in the physical, sexual union is to remind both partners of the even more remarkable oneness that the human spirit experiences with God in spiritual new birth when they put their trust in Jesus (John 3).

So sex is a good gift—but also a dangerous gift. It must be handled with care both before and after marriage. What are some principles that should shape our heart, and mold our minds that allow Christ to be glorified in our sex lives (1 Corinthians 6:18–20; 10:31)?

First, remember that God made us sexual creatures and gave us sex as one of His good gifts. He fitted us perfectly for heterosexual union and designed us to enjoy this coming together in sexual union within covenantal marriage.

Second, because sex is to take place within the covenant of marriage, any sex outside of marriage is sinful and wrong. This would include premarital sex, extramarital sex, and unnatural sex such as homosexuality.

Third, sex is a powerful passion that can override both the mind and the will. Simply put, it does not matter how much you love Jesus: the wrong person + the wrong time + the wrong place = the wrong thing happening. The Bible teaches that David was a man after God's heart (Acts 13:22), but as a result of being with the wrong person at the wrong time in the wrong place—as a result of committing adultery—David went on to lie, betray a friend, and murder. Acting on His truly amazing grace, God did forgive David's sin, but his life was never the same.

Fourth, God tells us to save ourselves for marriage and to be faithful in marriage in order to maximize several blessings. These blessings include partnership, pleasure, and protection. According to the experts, those who marry as virgins and stay true to their marriage covenant—those who use the gift as the Giver intends—will enjoy sex better, and they will never fear contracting an STD.

Fifth, put in place some wise parameters and guardrails that will help you maintain sexual purity and fidelity. Here are six:

1. Guard your thought life (Proverbs 23:7; Romans 12:2).
2. Guard your eyes (Job 31:1; Proverbs 20:12).
3. Watch your hands, your pelvic area, and your mouth when dating (1 Corinthians 6:18).
4. Never be alone with someone of the opposite sex except your spouse. Always make sure there are people around.
5. Never do anything when dating that you would not be willing to do in a room full of people.
6. Never do when dating what you would not want done to or with your future mate.

Sixth, recognize that viewing pornography will scar your mind and give you a jaundiced view of humans made in God's image and what healthy sex really is. Porn is a cesspool that will take you where you do not want to go. Sorrow, heartache, and frustration are its inevitable and constant companions.

Seventh, while "true love does wait," true love for Jesus is to drive our sexual ethics. God has not called us just to abstinence. He has called us to purity both in thought and action. As we pursue Christ, as we find our satisfaction and contentment in Him, we are freed to serve and honor others. The idea of using others ("friends with benefits") and exploiting others (sexual abuse) will evaporate in the brightness of His glory and goodness. Our goal is to treat others the way Christ has treated us: in accordance with God's will, with grace, and with love. This is the path to a wonderful sex life on which God will smile.

No Sex Until Marriage?

JORDAN EASLEY
Long Hollow Baptist Church, Hendersonville, TN

We human beings have a tendency to push boundaries . . .

When I was sixteen years old, I got pulled over for speeding. When the officer told me I was going seventy-two in a seventy zone, I looked at him and said, "I was only going two miles an hour over the speed limit. Can you just give me a warning?" He pulled his sunglasses down, looked me in the eye, and said, "You need to learn that seventy means seventy, and if you don't learn that as a sixteen-year-old, you're going to end up hurting yourself or someone else."

In the same way, we tend to push the boundaries with God when it comes to the subject of sex, and the reason is pretty simple: God created us as sexual beings who have natural desires. And He gave us sexual desire for a couple of reasons:

1. **To bring children into the world:** God commanded, "Be fruitful and multiply," and Adam and Eve's response was an emphatic, "Great plan! We're willing to obey You on this one!"

2. **To experience intimate companionship:** This intimate companionship with one another is what the Bible refers to as "becoming one flesh."

It's natural for us to desire sex, but sex doesn't just come from your hormones. Sex comes from God. Sex was God's idea, His plan. We tend to ruin many of God's perfect plans, and sex is no exception.

God gave us sex as a gift, and with the gift came guidelines. He put a speed limit sign up and expected us to obey the law. But we are pushing the limits.

The statistics show that roughly 63 percent of teenagers in America, ages fourteen through nineteen, are sexually active right now—and, sadly, church-going teenagers are included in this statistic.

The Bible is clear about sex. *Sex* and *sexual purity* are referenced over four hundred times in Scripture (Romans 13:13; Colossians 3:5; Hebrews 13:4).

Now, understand that sex is not the problem. Sex is great! It's awesome! It's a gift from God! It's beautiful—*if* it's sex according to His rules outlined in His Word. It's amazing—*if* it takes place between one man and one woman for one lifetime. Sex is not the problem; sexual sin is the problem.

To be specific, adultery is the problem, and adultery isn't only a married man sleeping around on his wife. Adultery is any sexual activity outside the union of marriage, and that includes sex before marriage. First Corinthians 6:18 reads, "Run from sexual sin!" (NLT). Don't flirt with the boundaries to see how far you can go and still get away with it.

We live in a world that is morally collapsing, and people are playing around with sex like it's just a form of entertainment.

That's why God commands, "Clothe yourself with the presence of the Lord Jesus Christ" (Romans 13:14 NLT). When you let that happen, you'll find it easier to answer many questions you have about sex.

Many people ask the question, "How far is too far?" When Christ is in charge of your life, answering that question is easier. After all, your body is not your own; it's another gift from God. And God sees your body as a holy temple (1 Corinthians 6:19). So your body isn't yours to share with whomever you want; your body is on loan for the purpose of bringing glory to God. No wonder He commands us to "run away from anything that stimulates youthful lusts" (2 Timothy 2:22 NLT).

When I began dating my wife, I was sixteen years old, 5'9" tall, and 130 pounds. Her dad was an intimidating 6'3" and 225 pounds, but he wasn't always with us. At times I was alone with his daughter—or was I? The Bible teaches that we serve an omnipresent God. That means that God, the Creator of the universe, is always with us. He sees and knows everything we do.

So, how far is too far when you're on a date? Here's a good idea: make the commitment to not do anything alone with your boyfriend/girlfriend that you wouldn't do in front of your parents. If I had tried to touch my girlfriend in an inappropriate place in front of her dad, I wouldn't be writing this. I'd be buried six feet under somewhere in West Texas.

It's wise to establish rules while your clothes are on and you're thinking clearly. Here are a few more suggestions:

* Rule 1: Don't unbutton, unzip, untie, unsnap, un-Velcro any clothing item.
* Rule 2: Don't lie down with your date or be behind closed doors alone.
* Rule 3: Don't touch anywhere where there is underwear—or where underwear is supposed to be.
* Rule 4: When you get married, forget rules 1, 2, and 3.

God's not trying to be a killjoy. His rules are for your good, and His rules often come with a promise—as we see here: "God's will is for you to be holy, so stay away from all sexual sin. Then each of you will control his own body and live in holiness and honor" (1 Thessalonians 4:3–5 NLT).

When I was fourteen, I made a commitment to God and to myself that I would be sexually pure until my wedding night. In another church about five miles down the road, the woman God had picked out for me was making the very same commitment.

God allowed me to meet my wife when I was sixteen. We dated for four and a half years, we maintained a pure relationship before our wedding day, and God has blessed us immensely.

Don't get me wrong! It was tough to stay sexually pure. Satan attacks Christians, especially if you've made a commitment to Christ to abstain from sex. But at the same time, God gives you the ability to keep His command-ments, and He blesses you when you do.

Born This Way

RIC GARLAND
Word of Life Fellowship, Schroon Lake, NY

Lady Gaga's song "Born This Way" hit the airwaves in 2011. Her song addresses the issue of people's equality regardless of skin color, beliefs, and, yes, sexuality. Although, when we listen to the lyrics, Lady Gaga may be speaking more of God's truth than she realizes . . .

Here is a brief summary of the gay perspective prevalent today:

"HOMOSEXUALITY IS AN ALTERNATIVE AND MORAL SEXUAL ORIENTATION."

* Being gay is a matter of sexual orientation that one is born with *genetically*; homosexuality is not a *choice.*
* Since I was created a homosexual, then it must be a normal and natural alternative lifestyle.
* If this natural lifestyle is not a choice, then homosexuality is a minority lifestyle, and their civil rights should receive the same protection extended to all other minorities.

Now let's look at the biblical perspective:

"HOMOSEXUALITY IS AN IMMORAL SEXUAL ORIENTATION PROHIBITED BY GOD."

* Homosexuality is clear violation of God's design.
* Since homosexuality violates God's design, it is a sin, and sin is always destructive. Homosexual behavior can destroy everyone involved.
* Then homosexuality is therefore a moral issue as well as a civil matter.

Let's look at the real issue at the core of this hot-button topic. And that real issue is "What is sin?"

Sin has been defined as anything that does not conform to the glory of God. That is the standard against which sin is measured in the familiar verse Romans 3:23.[1]

The Bible clearly teaches that homosexuality is sin (Romans 1:24, 26–27; 1 Corinthians 6:9–10). (By the way, so is sex before marriage, adultery, and every other deviation from God's plan for sex.)

The Bible also clearly teaches that we are all *born* sinners. Our sin nature—we sin because we're sinners; we're not sinners because we sin—goes back to Adam, who made the choice that now affects us all. One effect is that we can sin in a multitude of ways (1 Corinthians 6:12–20).

In the sense that (Fact #1) homosexuality is sin and (Fact #2) we are all born sinners, then, yes, homosexual individuals were born this way. (Are you tracking, Lady Gaga? Keep reading.) We are all born sinners—and sin isn't natural or normal.

Again, all of us are *born* sinners and each one of us *chooses* to sin, but each of us has our own propensities toward different sins.

So, Lady Gaga was on to something: we are born this way. What Lady Gaga doesn't realize is that we need a Savior to rescue us from our sinfulness, from the propensities toward sin with which we are born, and from our choices to sin.

In light of the arguments we just reviewed, how should we respond to our gay friends?

> All of us are *born* sinners and each one of us *chooses* to sin, but each of us has our own propensities toward different sins. **>**

1. SEPARATE THE SINNER FROM THE SIN.

God hates sin, but He loved all of us "while we were still sinners" (Romans 5:8). The principle of "love the sinner, but hate the sin" applies here. Homosexuality is just one small part of who your friends are. They are also sinners just like you, sinners in need of a Savior.

2. SHARE TRUTH IN LOVE (EPHESIANS 4:15).

And for unbelievers, the issue is not the homosexuality but that they are sinners and they need a Savior.

When talking with homosexual believers, your approach is different: clearly and lovingly share God's explicit Word. Explain that their new nature in Christ frees them from being enslaved to the propensities they have had. They—like you, whatever your all-too-frequent sins—are able to choose not to sin because the Holy Spirit dwells within us.

3. GIVE HOPE.

First Corinthians 6:11 offers the hope all of us sinners need: "You were washed, but you were sanctified, but you were justified in the name of the Lord Jesus and by the Spirit of our God."

4. KEEP THE FOCUS NOT ON HUMAN BEINGS BUT ON GOD AND HIS PLAN.

Homosexuality is a hot topic. Calm discussions of the issue are rare, and people arguing from both extremes make it difficult for us to share God's truth. But if we have decided to allow God's Word—rather than human logic or other people's opinions—to be the foundation for our lives, we can also rely on His Spirit to go before us into conversations; to soften the hearts of the people we talk with, to enable us to speak clearly, lovingly, and effectively; and to use the life-giving seeds of truth, forgiveness, and grace that we sow.

It's a Brain Changer

DENNIS STEEGER
Grace Outreach, Plano, TX

I t is impossible to accurately gauge the impact that pornography has on individuals, families, society, and culture. Its devastating power is both colorblind and equal opportunity in regard to gender, religious beliefs, socio-economic status, age, and position in life. For all of the ills it brings on society, pornography most severely impacts individuals and marriages.

There can be little doubt that pornography is hazardous to our health. Pornography is a cancer to our character. It destroys our virtue, it corrupts our goodness, and it dulls our moral sensibilities. Pornography ultimately affects our relationships, our attitudes, and our ability to be faithful to our spouse. It is all too easy to underestimate the negative effects of pornography, but its powerful ability to enslave is a danger we cannot afford to ignore.

While the most recent statistics tell us that nearly as many women are viewing porn as men, its impact on men seems much more profound. Men seem to be wired in such a way that pornography hijacks the proper functioning of our brain and has a long-lasting effect on our thoughts and, ultimately, our lives.

> Pornography is a cancer to our character. >

Some have said, "Pornography isn't really that bad. It's just something I play with." The problem is, porn is not a plaything; it is a pathway. New research indicates that when a man watches pornography, something actually changes in his brain. Pornography actually changes the neural pathways in our mind, creating powerful strongholds and hard-to-break habits.

As men become more deeply involved in pornography and more obsessed by these images, that exposure creates neural pathways. Over time these "neural paths become wider as they are repeatedly traveled with each and every exposure to pornography."[1] The paths our thoughts travel become more entrenched, locking us into a pattern of thinking. They become the conduit through which our interactions with women are processed. Consequently, "every woman they come into contact with is objectified, undressed and evaluated as a willing (or unwilling) mental sexual partner."[2]

While this may illustrate the biological nature of the male brain, the "my brain made me do it" does not constitute a get-out-of-jail-free card. (Our biology is not an excuse for our sins!) To break pornography's strongholds, we must begin to reclaim our purity. Unfortunately, sin does not give up easily, nor does it relinquish its hold on us without a struggle. Its impact on our lives is profound, and its teachings are powerful.

Specifically, pornography teaches us all the wrong lessons about sex. Within the context of marriage, sex is the ultimate act of commitment. It is the consummation of a "till death do us part" relationship. Every time a husband and wife come together in this manner, they are using their bodies to restate the love and affection they have for each other and to reaffirm the commitment they have made to each other. Within the confines of marriage, sex builds commitment, trust, and intimacy.

Pornography, however, takes us in a completely different direction. Pornography teaches us that real bodies aren't sufficient to satisfy our physical and emotional desires. Pornography also teaches us that one body alone cannot satisfactorily fulfill us. Finally, the most devastating lesson pornography will teach is not so much a lesson for me, but for my future wife—and it will be a painful lesson indeed. Pornography will teach her that she isn't sufficient, that she cannot satisfy me, and that she isn't good enough.

Unfortunately, we've seen a generation of marriages destroyed by a lack of faithfulness to one's vows. Is it possible that viewing pornography is equal to being unfaithful to our future spouse? Jesus said if a man looks at a woman with lust in his heart he has *already committed* adultery. Sex, therefore, in the mind of God, is not just a physical act, but it is also a mental act. Jesus said committing sex with our minds is equal to having sex with our bodies. So we must pay careful attention to what we watch and what we hear. What we choose may open doors to sexual immorality.

Purity, however, cultivates a capacity for faithfulness. So we must develop a purity filter for our eyes. Purity is not only physical; it's also mental and spiritual in its very nature. A single look at Bathsheba sent King David's moral compass into a spin!

In Psalm 51:10, David cried out, "Create in me a clean heart, O God." David desired to be cleansed of the impurities of his heart and the corruption of his mind. What David saw with his eyes had motivated his sinful actions. These actions so devastated David's life, that, in a moment of repentance and clarity, he cried out to God.

The only way for a young man to keep his way pure is to live according to God's Word. We would be wise to heed the words of Job: "I have made a covenant with my eyes not to look lustfully at a young woman" (31:1 NIV). We men must control where our eyes wander.

The bottom line is this: if you think about something long enough, if you persistently engage in the mental process of a specific behavior, you will eventually act on those things that you are thinking about. So where do you spend most of your mental time? Choose instead—by the power of the Holy Spirit—to follow the command God spoke through Paul: "Whatever things are true, whatever things are noble, whatever things are just, whatever things are pure, whatever things are lovely, whatever things are of good report, if there is any virtue and if there is anything praiseworthy—meditate on these things" (Philippians 4:8). It is time for us to think seriously about what we are thinking about.

Far-Reaching Consequences

RON COONEY
Calvary Baptist Church, Clearwater, FL

I will set nothing wicked before my eyes.

—PSALM 101:3

I was twelve years old when I came across two boxes in my father's room. He had recently cleaned out my late uncle's apartment and brought back with him a collection of magazines from the fifties and sixties. I knew I'd stumbled across something I wasn't supposed to find as I began flipping through the pages. I felt hypnotized by the images. For the first time in my life, I was exposed to pornographic material.

Like David on his rooftop (2 Samuel 11), I foolishly put myself in a situation that I wasn't prepared to face. On that summer day, I did not look for what I found, but I found what I was looking for. Read that again out loud. I wasn't looking for porn. I was snooping around my father's room hoping to find something I wasn't supposed to, and guess what? I found it. I just didn't realize the long-lasting hold that decision would have on me.

> Your choices today affect your tomorrows. >

CHOICES FOR TODAY, CONSEQUENCES FOREVER

It's a simple fact: your choices today affect your tomorrows. So you have to learn to make decisions now that will get you where you want to go. For example, if you want to play football in college, you should *choose* to play football in high school, work out with a trainer, and study hard. You should also choose *not* to do certain things like smoke cigarettes, experiment with drugs, or worry about your social life. Regular attention to these seemingly insignificant choices will make it easier for you to accomplish your bigger decision to play football at the collegiate level.

Most of you reading this book are going to choose to get married, and then you will likely want to be a faithful spouse and a good parent. God wants your marriage to be a reflection of Christ and His church (Ephesians 5:21–33) and your family to bring honor and glory to Him. He wants you to raise your children to learn about the salvation Jesus offers them. And pornography is one of the most deadly threats to being a family that honors Jesus.

Referring back to my own experience, I'll explain what involuntarily goes on in your body when you look at porn. As I began to flip through the pages of those magazines, a signal was being sent to my adrenal glands saying, "This is good stuff! I want more!" A hormone called epinephrine was released into my bloodstream during this emotional high that locked the magazine images into my brain—and twenty years later I still vividly remember them.[1] My decision on that fateful day impacted my tomorrows, and I carry that with me today as a husband and a father.

Maybe some of you reading this have already begun to experience the destructive nature of this addiction. Maybe you live in constant fear that someone has been in your room while you were out. You wonder if your parents have been on your computer or phone and are ready to expose you. Basically, you are finding yourself a slave to your own sin (John 8:34).

WHERE IS GOD?

The good news is that you don't have to stay a slave because God has provided you with a path out of the pit. In John 8:35–36, Jesus said, "The slave does not remain in the house forever; the son remains forever. So if the Son sets you free, you will be free indeed" (esv). You must understand that Christ is the only One who can set you free from this sin. You cannot merely will your way to restoration.[2] Christ must be the Physician, or there will be no cure.

> **Christ is the only One who can set you free from this sin. >**

As a Christian, you show your love for God by obeying Him (John 14:15). The Bible contains His commands—the standards by which you live your life (Psalm 119:9–10)—as well as the prescription for your healing. So where does the Bible tell us to start? You might think that God wants you to fight off this sin, but He actually requires the opposite. God commands, "Flee sexual immorality" (1 Corinthians 6:18). Your body was made to glorify God. So, whatever "it" is, throw it away, turn it off, take it out, or trade it in!

Once you have eliminated the threat, you need to repent of your sin. Repentance includes turning from sin and pursuing God. It isn't enough to turn your back on sin; you must move toward God (2 Timothy 2:22). You might also find that you need to break off certain relationships. Replace those with two or three adults you can trust to listen and direct you. Accountability isn't primarily about your "problem"; accountability challenges you and reminds you to press into Jesus and increase your dependence upon Him.

Finally, and most importantly, develop the habit of spending time with God in prayer and Bible study. The path to renewal is meditating and memorizing God's Word: "Do not be conformed to this world, but be transformed by the renewing of your mind" (Romans 12:2). Pray that God will replace your hunger for sexually immoral things with an even stronger passion to bring Him glory through the study of His Word. By consistently fleeing from pornography, repenting of your sin, and spending time with God, you will know what it is like to have God's grip tighten (John 10:28–29) while your sin's grip loosens its hold.

ADDITIONAL RESOURCES

* www.XXXChurch.com

SCRIPTURES FOR MEDITATION

* Colossians 2:6–15
* Colossians 3:1–3
* 1 Corinthians 6:12–20
* Galatians 5:16
* Psalm 119:9–10
* James 5:16
* 1 John 1:9–10
* Romans 12:1–2

> God commands, "Flee sexual immorality." >

Responding with Love

MICHAEL HEAD
Second Baptist Houston, Houston, TX

In just five hours, Lady Gaga obliterated the iTunes record for fastest-selling single with her song "Born This Way." It became the #1 song in over twenty-one countries and sold 1.1 million records in one week! These statistics tell me two things:

1. Our culture agrees with what Lady Gaga is saying about homosexuals.
2. Lady Gaga is using her voice to advance her message.

Homosexuality has become the norm. Every day hundreds of people "come out of the closet," and our culture doesn't even react. TV shows, songs, movies, books, magazines, radio stations, and celebrities have all helped our society become numb to and therefore accepting of the homosexual lifestyle. Even churches today are not willing to preach truth because they are afraid of hurting the feelings of the homosexual community. Although Scripture's teachings on the subject are clear, the church has softened its stance and relegated homosexuality to the status of "the ignored sin."

But consider what does the Bible says about homosexuality—and how strong those statements are. The Old Testament is very straightforward: "Do not practice homosexuality, having sex with another man as with a woman. It is a detestable sin" (Leviticus 18:22 NLT). God established a distinct order in His creation: He made a woman the perfect complement for a man, and a man the perfect complement for a woman. A man and a woman united in marriage reflects God's design for the family, His perfect order for the human race. Single moms and single dads can do a great job of raising their kids alone, but God has designed the family to function best with a mom and a dad. Boys need male role models in their life who can show them how to treat a woman, and girls need female role models as well as a father whose love helps mold her into a beautiful and confident young lady. Kids need both a dad and a mom, a male and a female, for the best chance of growing up emotionally healthy. Why would that be true? Simply because that's the way God designed the family.

The New Testament teachings are as straightforward as those in the Old Testament:

> Neither the sexually immoral nor idolaters nor adulterers nor male prostitutes nor homosexual offenders nor thieves nor the greedy nor drunkards nor slanderers nor swindlers will inherit the kingdom of God. (1 Corinthians 6:9–10 NIV)

> Although they knew God, they neither glorified him as God nor gave thanks to him, but their thinking became futile and their foolish hearts were darkened. . . . God gave them over to shameful lusts. Even their women exchanged natural relations for unnatural ones. In the same way the men also abandoned natural relations with women and were inflamed with lust for one another. Men committed indecent acts with other men, and received in themselves the due penalty for their perversion. (Romans 1:21, 26–27 NIV)

Throughout its pages, the Bible teaches in no uncertain terms that homosexuality is a sin. Nowhere does it ever say that homosexuality is a good thing or something we can overlook. We who are believers in Jesus Christ should know what the Bible says about sin and be ready—as Lady Gaga was—to use our voice to share that message. If we don't, our silence could push someone deeper into the trap of sin.

Although we who know God's Word disagree with Lady Gaga wholeheartedly, we can learn from her technique. Lady Gaga has used her voice to take a stand, giving unfounded peace to people struggling with homosexuality and perhaps other sins as well. We must follow Gaga's example: find a sense of urgency, use our voice, and communicate our message. After all, our message is the most amazing message ever. It's the gospel, the good news of Jesus' love and His death on the cross for people's sins. We should be using our voice to draw people to Jesus. He came to earth to show us how much He loves us: He came and died for all of our sick, disgusting sin. And we should treat homosexuals the way Jesus treated us: with 100 percent love. Here's the guideline from Jesus Himself: "You shall love your neighbor as yourself" (Mark 12:31).

> **We must love homosexuals with the love of Jesus. >**

We must love homosexuals with the love of Jesus. After all, homosexuals who act on those homosexual feelings are sinning just as you and I sin when we act on our feelings of anger, jealousy, or impatience. When any one of us acts in any way that is against God, we are sinning. All of us on this planet are sinners (Romans 3:23).

And we who are believers are called to love people, but we are not to love homosexuals or anyone else, whatever their sin, by affirming sinful choices that could keep them in bondage and prevent them from ever truly trusting in Christ. We must love by speaking the truth, but speaking the truth in love, not condemnation.

Jesus showed us exactly how to do this. Think about the woman caught in adultery (John 8). Jesus did not put her down; nor did He tell her that her lifestyle was okay. Instead, He spoke to her with love: " 'Neither do I condemn you,' Jesus declared. 'Go now and leave your life of sin' " (John 8:11 NIV).

Jesus recognized her sin and called it what it was: sin. Then, speaking in love, He told her to leave her sin. That is true love. Jesus definitely doesn't want us living in our sins and suffering the consequences of those sins. He wants us to turn from sin and walk in freedom. Relying on the strength of

Jesus Christ, you and I can overcome our sins. Also relying on the strength of Jesus Christ, homosexuals can leave their life of sin as well. Overcoming starts with first establishing a relationship with Jesus Christ and then getting help to continue to defeat that sin.

We are not to love by affirming sinful choices. >

Putting on the Armor of God

KEITH HARMON
Cross Church, Springdale, AR

Working with students like you for the past nineteen years has been one of the greatest joys in my life and at the same time it has been extremely heart wrenching.

Nineteen years ago young people were making decisions about what movie to see on the weekend, whom to ask to the prom, what cassette tape to buy for their Walkman, and whether they like Dr. Pepper or Coke better. Today you are being forced earlier and more often to make adult decisions. Thirteen-year-old students are dealing with issues that eighteen-year-old students used to face. I have seen a major shift in what young people are exposed to and how early they are exposed.

Of great concern to me is the fact that students today are constantly bombarded with sex and sexuality from every direction. You can't turn on the television, the radio, or your computer without some message about sex or some sexual image being right there in your face. You have to decide what you believe about sex, homosexuality, and marriage before you even get close to getting your driver's license. If young people like you don't turn to God and His Word for guidance on these issues, God alone knows where our culture will be in twenty years. Clearly, the Word of God must be our ultimate authority on these issues, on every critical issue that we—adults and young people alike—face on a daily basis. All of us are in a battle, and it's a battle for our hearts and minds.

Consider that the world says, "Do whatever you want," "Do what feels good," "Go with the flow," and "Do what makes sense." God says, "If you love Me, keep My commandments" (John 14:15); "You can identify people by their actions" (Matthew 7:18 NLT); and "Be holy, for I am holy" (1 Peter 1:15–16). The world's message and God's seem to contradict each other in major ways. Their messages about sex, for instance, could not be more opposite. Young people are hearing so many different messages from so many different sources that many of you don't know what to believe. In fact, many students I talk with aren't even sure what sex is. They don't believe, for instance, that oral sex, masturbation, fondling, groping, and anal sex are even sex. They don't see the danger of pornography. And too many times they'll say, "I am a technical virgin." (Do you see yourself anywhere in this mirror?)

All of us are in a battle. >

Well, I don't believe that Jesus plays games with semantics. He looks at the heart. He tells us that if we even look at someone with lust in our hearts, we have committed adultery with that person (Matthew 5:28). Another passage I often share with young people is this one:

> Flee sexual immorality. Every sin that a man does is outside the body, but he who commits sexual immorality sins against his own body. Or do you not know that your body is the temple of the Holy Spirit who is in you, whom you have from God, and you are not your own? For you were bought at a price: therefore glorify God in your body. (1 Corinthians 6:18–20)

These verses are a great reminder that our bodies are not our own to do with whatever we want. They belong to Jesus: He purchased them with His blood. Therefore, we are to glorify God with our body.

Whatever the areas of temptation you struggle most with—sex, gossip, disrespect, dishonesty, impatience—the spiritual battle rages. It only makes sense that we would arm ourselves for that battle by putting on the "whole armor of God" (Ephesians 6:11). What I do—and what I would encourage you to do—is to read Ephesians 6:10–20 each and every morning. After you have read this passage of Scripture, think about each piece of the armor: the belt of truth, the breastplate of righteousness, the gospel of peace, the shield of faith, the helmet of salvation, and the sword of the Spirit. And then pray!

Pray on each piece of the armor. As I pray on each piece, I touch those places on my body that the given piece is designed to protect. When I pray on the helmet of salvation, I touch my head and ask the Lord to protect my mind, my ears, and my eyes. When I put on the breastplate of righteousness, I touch my chest and ask the Lord to guard my heart. When I put on the belt of truth, I touch my waist and ask the Lord to help me be a man of integrity and speak truth today. I pick up the shield of faith and ask the Lord to give me incredible faith for that day. I then take up the sword of the Spirit and ask the Lord to speak directly to my heart through His Word. Every morning I go through these steps, and this practice of putting on each and every piece of armor has made a huge difference in my life. I encourage you to do this each and every day because the battle truly is 24/7.

And our enemy is powerful. Ephesians 6:12 tells us that we are not fighting "against flesh and blood, but against principalities, against powers, against the rulers of the darkness of this age, against spiritual hosts of wickedness in the heavenly places." Clearly, the devil wants to steal, kill, and destroy us (John 10:10). We are living that reality. But let's remember the truth from God's Word: when we put on the armor God provides, we are "able to stand against the wiles of the devil" (Ephesians 6:11).

#family

Caring for the Victims of Divorce

DON LOUGH
Word of Life Fellowship, Schroon Lake, NY

I n America today, we face the pandemic of divorce. On any given night, 40 percent of American children go to sleep without a father in their home. Broken families have become the new normal. Yet divorce doesn't just shatter families; it shatters the lives of individuals who are caught in the crossfire. I'm talking about children of divorce, and maybe you're one. If not, you undoubtedly know several.

Tragically, children of divorce commonly struggle with issues like poor self-image, anger, fear of abandonment, emotional volatility, and shame. It is not uncommon for these students to conclude that they are the reason for their parents' divorce. Add to this the reality that some children of divorce are forced to make impossible decisions about which parent to live with and which house to call home. It's no wonder that God "hates divorce" (Malachi 2:16).

> Children of divorce commonly struggle with issues like poor self-image, anger, fear of abandonment, emotional volatility, and shame. >

So what can you do to help friends who are victims of divorce? (Know that these same principles apply if you yourself are a victim.) A natural response is to offer comfort and to try to put a hedge around them to cushion them from any further pain or hurt. But you can also help them—or find someone else who can help them—learn from the experience so they will not repeat the same patterns in their own marriage. Children of divorce also need to understand and embrace the sure promises of our steadfast God despite parents who have cast aside their commitments and broken their promises.

HELP YOUR FRIEND FIND A SAFE PLACE

Many children of divorce feel like home is a combat zone. Students dealing with their parents' divorce need a safe place to run when the conflict around them escalates. Inviting a friend into your own home is a simple thing that will, in many cases, have a profound and lasting impact. By the way, note how the string of greetings found in Romans 16 indicates that the apostle Paul deliberately stepped into the details of people's lives. He made himself available both for the highs and lows and became like family to many. While it's true that you will never replace a family member who is now distant because of the divorce, you can step into the void and give your friends some measure of security.

HELP REPLACE A MISSING SENSE OF VALUE

One of the most common consequences of divorce is a child's depleted sense of value—or, at the very least, confusion about the source of their value. Children lean so heavily on their parents for their identity and sense of worth. Absent or distracted parents aren't able to provide that vital affirmation. Yet students impacted by divorce need to know that they are valuable, and they need to hear the reasons why. You can't just tell them once and consider it done. Surround your friends with encouragement from every direction. Speak God's truth to them, write it down, and celebrate it. Remind them of the profound truths of Psalm 139: they are "fearfully and wonderfully made" by God (v. 14), and He is intimately interested in their lives. Also make sure your friends know that God values them regardless of their performance, yet make a big deal of spiritual successes. Help your hurting friends learn that God is pleased by the trust they place in Him.

HELP STUDENTS LEARN HOW TO FORGIVE

When their family has been ripped apart by divorce, your friends' survival will ultimately rest on their ability to forgive. Of course this is not always easy, but it is always and absolutely necessary. In fact, you will need to guard your own heart as you uncover the anguish of your hurting friends.

> Make sure your friends know that God values them. >

Remember the parable of the unforgiving servant that Jesus told (Matthew 18:21–35). No matter how much a person has been wronged, he or she has been forgiven so much more. The roots of forgiveness grow in the soil of gratitude for this divine forgiveness. So help your friends realize how much God has forgiven them for and then prompt them to extend a measure of that same forgiveness to their parents. The goal is to help your friends arrive at a position of genuine respect and love for both parents.

Think about friends who are walking through a divorce. God may have strategically placed you in their life for such a time as this: to walk beside them through the pain and the difficulty. By His grace and in His power, you can do exactly that.

Growing Up with Absent Parents

JEREMY NOTTINGHAM
First Baptist Church, Broken Arrow, OK

She sat on the other side of my desk, weeping, as she told me about the strained relationship she had with her dad. She had been one of the leaders in our youth ministry before she began to bounce from boyfriend to boyfriend, from one inappropriate relationship to the next. She was sixteen years old, and I'll never forget what she said: "I have zero relationship with my dad, so I'm trying to fill this hole in my heart with these guys. They're the only ones who tell me I'm pretty and say that they love me."

Absent fathers, stepparents, two homes, and brokenhearted teenagers have become the norm in student ministries. And this breakdown of the family is the root of so many other issues. If young people don't have a solid family—and you've undoubtedly seen this and perhaps even experienced it—they run to things like alcohol, drugs, cutting, pornography, and eating disorders. And they run away from God.

In his book *Hurt*, Chap Clark writes about this subject of teenage abandonment, as he terms it. His in-depth research shows the desperate need that young people have for support and attention, especially from their parents and other adults. When teens do not receive support from parents, they look to other adults. Unfortunately, adults too often focus on those young people who are more gifted, better looking, or smarter. Clark writes, "The sharp and attractive and the rebellious and countercultural make up only 20 percent of the population, and yet they receive 80 percent of adults' attention."[1] Students who don't shine on the athletic field or in the classroom and students who aren't constantly in trouble are often the ones who suffer the most. And of that 80 percent, those who don't have support at home suffer even more. They feel

 85

abandoned at home, and it's unlikely they will receive positive reinforcement from coaches, teachers, and even youth pastors. This has to change.

I truly believe that this kind of abandonment is one of the most critical issues facing our culture today. Innocent young people—you and your friends—are having to deal with the consequences of their parents' sin, and these broken homes lead to so many other problems. If this abandonment issue could be solved, other issues could be solved as well.

> If you are caught in this painful world of abandonment, know that there is hope. >

But if you are caught in this painful world of abandonment, know that there is hope. Please don't give up. Hear Jesus' invitation to you: "Come to Me, all you who labor and are heavy laden, and I will give you rest. Take My yoke upon you and learn from Me, for I am gentle and lowly in heart, and you will find rest for your souls. For My yoke is easy and My burden is light" (Matthew 11:28–30). If your parents are either out of your home physically or out of your home mentally and emotionally because of a job, lean on Jesus. Jesus will provide for you and take care of you through the difficult and painful days you face. I also encourage you to find a strong church and youth ministry to get plugged in to. You need the support of other godly students and adults who love you and will walk with you. Understand that great days are ahead.

I know: this time is dark and may seem impossible, but I'll say it again: when you follow Christ, great days *are* ahead. Psalm 30:5 says, "Weeping may spend the night, but there is joy in the morning" (HCSB). And Romans 8:28 says, "We know that all things work together for the good of those who love God: those who are called according to His purpose" (HCSB). Your story and your struggle could be what God uses one day to change the life of someone facing a similar struggle. God can take a painful and horrible story of abandonment and turn it into a life-changing story that will bring Him glory for eternity. Never give up.

A postscript for parents: I challenge you to separate yourself from your own agenda for your kids and realize that they desperately need you and your time. Stay committed to your marriage. Teenagers need you to stay together. Those who have to bounce back and forth from home to home are tired of it and are struggling. They need a strong support system at home, and they need to know that you are committed to each other and to the family. And, parents, when you get a new job opportunity or promotion, pray hard to make sure this is what God wants. So often with new responsibility comes less time at home. Making more money is not worth losing your kids. Millions of teenagers feel abandoned because their parents are still chasing the American Dream. It's not worth it. Jobs and promotions can wait, but your kids cannot. They don't need more money, more clothes, or more video games. Your kids need you. So I pray that you moms and dads will stay committed to God and to each other and that you will model Jesus to your children.

#pain

Dealing with Doubt

DAVE EDWARDS
David Edwards Productions, Oklahoma City, OK

Your phone rings, and the caller's message takes your breath away. Or someone knocks on your door, and one look at her face tells you all you need to know. The doctor—or pastor or boss or dean—asks you to step into his office. At moments like these, when the unthinkable happens, trust can turn to doubt and confidence can be shaken.

Doubt, however, is not a lack of trust. The essence of doubt is being caught between two extremes—peace and fear, hope and hopelessness—and pulled in opposite directions in your spirit. This spiritual tug-of-war tests us as our circumstances assault our faith. Feeling powerless, we surrender to fear, which grows like a vine from the root of doubt.

So how are we to deal with doubt? To find the strength we need to defeat doubt, we have to return to some foundational truths that enable us to trust God. We must go back to the basics before going forward in renewed faith.

Jesus knew that life events would cause us to doubt: "In the world you will have tribulation; but be of good cheer, I have overcome the world" (John 16:33). Jesus had no illusions that the world was perfect or that we would never suffer. In fact, in this verse, He actually guaranteed that hard times would come: "In this world you will have trouble." Jesus knew the world was full of suffering, abuse, sickness, and death. Yet into this battle-weary world He was born, He was raised, and He ministered. The evil He encountered in this world didn't shake His faith in God. Not once did Jesus doubt.

And we are to follow Jesus' example, for He is the One who said, "I have overcome." His word cuts through doubt and frees us from questions. He lifts our focus from the pain and disappointment and moves our eyes to Him. Defeating doubt doesn't mean having the mysteries of life all figured out.

Rarely are there clean, simple explanations for our suffering or good answers to the question "Why?" There is, however, a rock-solid answer to the question "Whom do I turn to?" Turn to Jesus.

And when doubts arise, may these three truths about Jesus ring in your heart.

HE IS THE CHRIST

Look again at what Jesus said. With the word *I*, He identified Himself to us as the only One qualified to take on all the hurt in the world. He is the Christ, and the word *Christ* means "the anointed one," the One God appointed to bear the burden of our sins, to guide our steps, to provide comfort, hope, and purpose. Jesus is legit. He is the real deal. He is the Messiah. Jesus fulfilled every single one of the Old Testament predictions about the Messiah. But who do you believe He is? Is Jesus your Christ? When we accept Jesus as our Christ, we sow the seeds of a trust that allows us to live authentically even in the face of doubt. A deep trust that can stand in the face of doubt is grounded in the truth of who Christ is.

HE IS IN CONTROL

Jesus proclaimed, "I have overcome!" Regardless of how things appear to us, He is ruling from His throne. He is in control no matter what events have made you doubt. He has the last say. Jesus gives life, and He redeems all manner of hurt. Not once when He walked the earth did Jesus ever hurt anyone or cause someone to suffer. Instead, He drew near and reached out to people who were hurting and questioning. Jesus brought wholeness where there was suffering; hope where He found despair; freedom where people were trapped; and life where death appeared to reign—and He does the same today. So when circumstances look hopeless, we need to remember that Jesus has the last say. When we are wrestling with doubt, we must remember not to blame God. God is not the problem; He is the answer. God is not your enemy; He is your ally. The Gospels paint a picture of Jesus fighting for us when we cannot fight for ourselves. When we are at our weakest, He is strong. No matter what you are facing, Jesus has the last say. Jesus is in control.

> No matter what you are facing, Jesus is in control. >

HE IS COMMITTED

When we doubt, we can easily feel offended or let down by God. Doubt is hard and sometimes lonely, so it's easy to feel that God is mad, angry, unfair, disgusted, uninterested, and indifferent—but He's not any of those things. He is with you, and you can find courage in the resurrected Jesus, the One who was victorious over sin and death. By His Spirit, Jesus is with you in the middle of your trouble. He knows what you are facing, feeling, and fighting, and He has not left you alone. He is with you, and He will see you through this season. So take courage from your risen Lord. He has not forgotten you. Despite the struggles you face and the doubts that haunt, you are not alone.

Now take these three basic truths and pray them into your doubt:

> *Dear Jesus, I believe that You are the Christ. You are in control of all of history and of my life. And You are committed to Your sheep; You are committed to me.*

Allow these truths to sink deep into your heart. However powerless and filled with doubt you feel, the truth is that God is present with you in all His strength, He hears your prayers, and He will see you through (Isaiah 43:1–3). Finally, remember that trust is not to be determined by feelings, circumstances, or thoughts. Trust is to be based on Jesus. He is the Christ. He is in control. He is committed to you. Let these truths take you back to trust.

Facing Loss without Losing Faith

> MIKE CALHOUN
> Word of Life Fellowship, Schroon Lake, NY

God knows everything. I'm sure that you've heard that before, and you may have even said it to your friends or little sister before. But I want you to stop for a minute and think about what that really means.

* God has no need to learn. God knows all things instantly and effortlessly. God never had a teacher. He never went to school. Nobody teaches God (Isaiah 40:13–14). As humans, we know a great deal, but we don't know the future. God knows everything from the beginning to the end. He knows all the variables and possible scenarios, and none of it is a surprise to Him. Nothing ever happens behind God's back (Hebrews 4:13).

* God is never surprised. He is never amazed. He will never discover anything. One of my favorite writers, A. W. Tozer, said it this way: "No talebearer can inform on us, no enemy can make his accusation stick, and no skeleton can come tumbling out of some hidden closet to turn Him against us."[1] The Bible says that God loved us while we were "still sinners" (Romans 5:8). He knew everything that you were going to do in your lifetime when He made the decision to save you. He knew that, as a believer, you were going to fail sometimes. In light of all that, He still loved you enough to send Jesus to die in your place.

* God is wise in Himself. In other words, God does not gain wisdom from others. I talk to people I respect, and I gain wisdom from them. But God doesn't gain wisdom from any of us. God never has to have a study session or a strategy meeting. God is all-wise, and as such He cannot make a mistake. God's ways cannot be improved upon. God's wisdom is

perpetual. It never fades or goes away. God is able to accurately judge all things. He never has felt regret or uncertainty.

* God does not make mistakes. God never says, "Oh no!" or, "Oops!" And this is where the topic starts to get a little bit difficult.

If God knows everything (He does) and if God is all-wise (He is) and if God does not make any mistakes (He doesn't), then why does God allow bad things to happen? To that question there is no easy answer.

In His wisdom and His love for us, God has chosen to give us freedom. He is not selective with this gift. All people—saints and serial killers, patriots and hippies, Christians and atheists, Yankees and good ol' boys—*all* people are recipients of the God-given freedom to choose. Sometimes we choose to do things that directly hurt those around us. Sometimes, through no fault of our own, you and I experience today the lasting consequences of choices made by people who lived and died thousands of years before us .

Throughout Scripture, several different people (Job, Jeremiah, Habakkuk, and John the Baptist, to name a few) struggled with this question about why God allows bad things to happen—and they asked God about it. These individuals dared to question God about why He would allow pain and hardship to continue on earth. God responds to that question differently than you might imagine. He does not call down fire and brimstone to maim the doubting. Actually, God is never angered by an honest heart. God is happy when we trust Him with our doubts.

> God is happy when we trust Him with our doubts. >

God hears those questions, smiles, and then responds the same way every time: He points to Himself. He never tries to explain away our pain, but He does ask if we will trust Him without getting an explanation from Him. God responds to our *why* questions with a *who* answer. God is there. He sees. He is in control—even when we don't understand.

At some point in life, each one of us will encounter an injustice, a crisis, a tragedy, a situation that doesn't seem fair. And each one of us will be forced to choose whether

> God responds to our *why* questions with a *who* answer. **>**

we are willing to trust God even when the world doesn't make sense. At that time, will you be able to say, as David did in Psalm 34:1, "I will bless the LORD at all times"?

When your whole world falls apart, remember that everything you know about God is still true.

The Depression Epidemic

RON LUCE
Teen Mania, Garden Valley, TX

There is an epidemic running rampant through this country, infecting every teen in America to some degree and, like a plague, taking its toll.

This plague kills your dreams. It stifles your potential. It makes you feel worthless and paralyzed. It makes you feel like a loser, unloved and unwanted. Sometimes this plague kills.

This plague is called "inferiority."

According to suicide.org, approximately 20 percent of teens experience depression before they reach adulthood, and between 10 to 15 percent suffer from symptoms at any one time. A teen takes his or her own life every one hundred minutes; suicide is the third leading cause of death for young people ages fifteen to twenty-four.[1]

As a result of feeling so low, millions turn to alcohol, drugs, and pornography to numb the pain. A lot of effort has been spent trying to solve the teen drug/alcohol problem, but the only way to solve it is to solve the self-esteem problem.

A 2010 study showed that teens today are five times more likely to suffer depression than their peers were during the Great Depression. Experts pointed at pop culture's emphasis on the external—on guys being sports heroes, on girls looking like models—as being the major reason for the upswing.[2] It doesn't matter how you look on the outside if you feel worthless on the inside. You can buy the "right" clothes and hang with the "right" people, but still feel like junk on the inside. Sometimes even friends and family make us feel like a nothing. And unfortunately, too many people leave a church service believing that God thinks we are worms.

But—an important aside—James 4:10 says, "Humble yourselves before the Lord, and he will lift you up" (NIV). That's the kind of God He is! He lifts you up because you are so valuable to Him.

Still, with all these negative messages from the media, your family, your friends, and sometimes even your preacher, the evidence seems to speak for itself. So look at something Jesus said: " 'You shall love the LORD your God with all your heart, with all your soul, and with all your mind.' This is the first and great commandment. And the second is like it: 'You shall love your neighbor as yourself' " (Matthew 22:37–39).

Do you see that? Jesus says that loving your neighbor *as yourself* is almost as important as loving God with all of your heart, soul, and mind. It's the second greatest commandment in the Bible! Too many people, though, think this means that we are to love God, then love others, and finally love self. But that's not what Jesus said. He said to love others *as* you love yourself. That means you must love others equally as much as you love yourself. If you don't love yourself, you can't love others. You can try, but it won't really come across as love.

Hearing that we should "love ourselves" sounds strange and kind of prideful, but arrogance actually comes from low self-esteem. The arrogant person feels so low about himself that he tries to make others believe that he is really something marvelous. He does *not* love himself. If he did, he wouldn't feel like he had to prove himself to anyone.

Look at what Jesus told Peter about this. In Luke 5:8, Peter told Jesus, "Go away from me, Lord; I am a sinful man!" Peter had the same mentality that a lot of us do today: "Get away from me, Lord; I'm ugly, dirty, and worthless." We push God away when we realize He is holy and we aren't. But look at Jesus' response: "Don't be afraid; from now on you will catch men" (v. 10 NIV). Jesus was saying to Peter, "Don't push yourself away from Me. I have a great future for you. Now stand up! See yourself the way I see you. You are going to do great things for God!"

It is *not* a sin to love yourself. It is holy, right, and—according to Jesus—the most important thing after loving God! It is a sin to *not* love yourself.

> Choose to believe the truth that you are fearfully and wonderfully made. >

And this truth is the only cure for today's inferiority epidemic. Choose to believe the truth about yourself. God created you in His image and you are fearfully and wonderfully made (Psalm 139:13–14).

The choice is yours. You can believe Hollywood, or you can believe God. You can believe *Seventeen* magazine, or you can trust the Bible. It's your choice. The world runs you into the ground; God lifts you up. If you believe what the world says, then you're calling God a liar. You're saying, "I don't care what You say, Lord. I still believe I'm a loser."

So what do you do now? Start by repenting. Pray, "God, please forgive me for calling You a liar. I commit to believing the truth about myself that You've shown me in Your Word. Speaking that truth to myself, I will no longer allow my feelings or what the world says to dictate my worth. If You say I am valuable, I'm going to believe what You say. In Jesus' name, amen."

When you buy something at the store, in your mind, it's worth whatever you paid for it. God could have given all of the gold, silver, diamonds, and oil in the world to redeem you to Himself. But that wouldn't have been enough—not even close! When God decided what to pay for you, He brought His own Son onto the scene and shed His blood for you! That's how much you are worth to God: the blood of His only beloved Son!

God wants to use you to change the world. Don't let the disease of inferiority shut you down! Choose today to believe what God says about you. You will never be the same!

Down and Out?

KELLY KNOUSE
Idlewild Baptist Church, Lutz, FL

I recently did a Google search, and the results absolutely blew me away! Did you know that there are forty-seven different medications for depression? And that was just the first page I clicked on! I sat there in front of my computer reading these drug names, most of which I can't even pronounce: doxepin, clomipramine, nortriptyline, trazodone, perphenazine, isocarboxa—what?! And the list goes on and on.

We may have a little trouble pronouncing the names of those prescription drugs, but the real problem is the depression they treat. You have family members, friends, coaches, and teachers who have experienced the lows of life. Maybe you yourself have experienced some hard times. The low points in life are real, and they can make you feel like you're done, you're over it, you're tired and tired of life. So what's the answer? Upping the dosage of whatever medicine you're on, reading a self-help book, taking a yoga class, or listening to Dr. Phil?

If you're a Christian, the Lord has redeemed your life for His purpose. But despite that divine purpose, you may sometimes find yourself looking for something—a sermon, a verse—to help you get through the week, the day, the hour, or your next class. What do you do when your emotional and spiritual tank is empty? You could once again repeat Jeremiah 29:11, about God having great plans for your life and hope and a future. But when you don't have much hope about your future, that promise sounds pretty empty. So maybe you make flashcards of Isaiah 41:10—"Fear not, for I am with you." But what does that even mean when it feels like the walls of life are closing in on you?

As a follower of Jesus, I fear that we Christians have too many bumper-sticker Bible answers, but don't really understand how God's truth applies to our lives. What do those (too-familiar?) verses really mean to someone who is down and out? I don't know about you, but when I'm down, I don't need another flip "Hang in there!" or trite "Let go and let God." Well-meaning people we know may offer this kind of response, but what does the God who created our soul have to say about the weariness within? I believe the answer may be closer than you think.

Take a fresh look with me at a passage of Scripture that you may have read a thousand times before. You may well have memorized it. Psalm 23:3 reads, "He restores my soul." We know that this psalm talks about God as our Shepherd and, in this word picture, we are the sheep. I don't know if you've recently studied the behavioral habits of a sheep in zoology class, but sheep are pretty dumb animals. Sheep will wander: they walk away from their shepherd. Sheep will worry: they don't have any natural defense mechanisms, and they're pretty low on the food chain. Because sheep wander and because they can't defend themselves, they end up with a lot of wounds.

If you've never been able to see yourself in this passage of Psalm 23, take a minute to ask yourself some honest questions:

* In what ways have I wandered from my Shepherd? What holy things have I walked away from?
* What worries, if any, are keeping me paralyzed? What about my situation, if anything, feels hopeless?
* What wounds are draining the life right out of me?

Your honest answers to these questions may help you identify some reasons why you're feeling depressed. Maybe you have an impossible family situation, and there just seems to be no reason to hope it will get better. Or you may be dealing with feelings of abandonment due to the way some significant people have treated you. You may have hit a roadblock in your pursuit of the goals and plans you once had. Maybe you deal with loneliness every day because you haven't found anyone in your life you can share your burdens with. All these things can make life feel hopeless. Just like a sheep who falls, gets stuck on its back, and can't stand up without help, you can get stuck in your hopelessness.

So what do you do now? Psalm 23:3 says that the Lord your Shepherd wants to *restore* your soul so that you don't have to stay stuck.

1. ADMIT YOU NEED A GUIDE.

The rest of Psalm 23:3 says, "He guides me in paths of righteousness" (NIV). Isaiah 53:6 says that we are all like sheep who have wandered our own way. God, the Great Shepherd, wants to lovingly and gently guide you back to a place of spiritual awakening. Your part is to admit that you need Him. You were not created to do life alone. Ask your Shepherd for help and guidance.

2. EXPERIENCE THE POWER OF FORGIVENESS.

The enemy uses *condemnation* to keep us paralyzed. The Holy Spirit uses *conviction* to move us away from guilt and regrets to the freedom of forgiveness. Psalm 23:3 says that our good Shepherd guides us in "paths of righteousness." The shepherd doesn't merely scold the sheep when it wanders, but instead puts the sheep back on the right path. God wants you on a path of rightness with Him, and if you're feeling hopeless, somewhere along the way you got off the path.

3. TRUST GOD WHEN YOU DON'T UNDERSTAND.

Psalm 23:3 ends with "for His name's sake." We don't always understand the journey when we follow a guide—even when we follow the Guide in the journey of life—but we can trust the heart of our Shepherd-Guide. Remember that your circumstances are for His name, not yours. All that He allows you to experience is about bringing Him glory in your life.

If Life Is Getting Dark . . . for You or Someone You Know

> **KEITH HARMON**
> Cross Church, Springdale, AR

* On an average day, one person ends their life every seventeen minutes.
* Suicide takes the lives of about thirty thousand people each year.
* Every two hours and twelve minutes a teenager/young adult kills him- or herself.
* Among persons age fifteen to twenty-four, suicide is the third leading cause of death, behind accident and homicide.
* Persons under age twenty-five account for approximately 16 percent of all suicides.[1]

Darkness can get pretty dark, can't it?

If you can say yes from experience, I'm sorry—but I'm glad you're reading this.

First, I want to talk to those of you who have thought or are thinking about hurting yourself or taking your life—but even if you're not in that kind of desperate spot, read on. What you find may raise your compassion quotient as well as give you some insight for when you do meet someone who is all too familiar with darkness.

* "Here on earth you will have many trials and sorrows" (Jesus in John 16:33 NLT). No matter how often we've reminded ourselves of this truth, we can still be blindsided by the pain we experience in life. The intensity, the frequency, the injustice, the exhaustion, the "why?"—all this can be overwhelming. But if you're considering taking your own life, stop for a minute. Behind that thought is undoubtedly the desire to escape pain—pain that you never signed up for, pain beyond description. Let

  • • • • • • • • • • • • • • • • • • •

me reassure you that—even if you can't see them—options other than ending your life exist. Of course you want the pain to go away. Jesus wants your pain to go away too.

* But you may not want to hear *about* Jesus or *from* Jesus now. Pain can prompt that reaction. If you're willing to hear from Jesus—but even if you're not—know that He is saying this: "Come to Me, all you who . . . are heavy laden, and I will give you rest" (Matthew 11:28). He is there for you—and "I believe; help my unbelief" may be the perfect prayer for you at this point.

* Sometimes when we need Jesus, we can't go to Him under our own strength. Remember the paralytic whose four friends lowered him through the roof to the feet of Jesus? The Lord healed the man "when Jesus saw their faith" (Mark 2:5). Do you see that? Not the paralytic's faith, but his friends' faith. So if you can't go to Jesus on your own strength, let others do the heavy lifting for you. Let your friends take you—in prayer—to the Lord's feet. Every single believer on earth and throughout all time encounters seasons in life when we need to let others pray for us when we ourselves just can't pray, seasons in life when we need to let others believe in God's goodness and love and promises when we struggle to believe.

* Another reason to reach out to fellow believers is this: you are in a spiritual battle. Jesus wants to give you abundant life, but the enemy wants to take you out. Don't fight the devil by yourself. Again, reach out to just one person. He or she can rally the troops of prayer warriors.

* Right now you may feel like the rope in a tug-of-war between Jesus, the Life Giver, and Satan, the life taker. Recognize that any self-destructive or suicidal thought is not from Jesus, but from the evil one. And if you are a follower of Christ, Satan has no business messing with you. Remind

him of that truth by speaking out loud, "Satan, I am the Lord's. In the powerful name of Jesus, I command you to leave—and to leave me alone!"

Now, for those of you who want to come alongside a hurting friend . . .

* You don't have to fix anything. The truth is that you probably can't fix anything. You can listen—and God can use that gesture of Christlike compassion and kindness to shine some light into your friend's darkness. Again, you don't have to fix anything. Just listen. Don't try to solve. Don't speak clichés. Don't worry about quoting Scripture. You don't even need to pray out loud. Just be there.

* "Do unto others" may be a helpful guideline. Put a hand on the leg or an arm around the shoulders. Offer regular "um-hmms" and an occasional "I'm so sorry."

Also, be aware that you—or your friend—may need professional support. If your leg had been broken as long as your spirit has been . . . if a wound had been bleeding as long as your heart has been . . . you would have already been at the ER. So don't just "give it time." *Now* is the time. Maybe you know of a local resource, but if not, call this toll-free number, available twenty-four hours a day, every day: 1-800-273-TALK (8255). This National Suicide Prevention Lifeline is available to anyone. You may call for yourself or for someone you care about, and all calls are confidential.

The prophet Isaiah wrote that Jesus came to, among other things, "give a crown of beauty for ashes, a joyous blessing instead of mourning" (Isaiah 61:3 NLT). And your response is, "Lord, I believe; help my unbelief!" (Mark 9:24). That's okay. It counts as a mustard seed.

Short-Circuit Your Secret

> **DAVE EDWARDS**
> David Edwards Productions, Oklahoma City, OK

Pssst! Are you living with a secret? The presence of a secret brings with it the fear of being found out. What is your secret? Is it an addiction? Abuse? Jealousy? Insecurity? Dishonesty?

You didn't start out with secrets. Prior to the birth of every secret was the choice to hide truth because of pain or fear. You did something or something happened to you. Suddenly everything was different—and you had a secret. It may feel like the lights went out, and now part of you is living in the dark. What will you do with your secret?

God's Word gives you a way out of hiding and a path back into the light. Take a moment to read Proverbs 28:13–14 below. Read it slowly so the words sink in: "He who covers his sins will not prosper, but whoever confesses and forsakes them will have mercy. Happy is the man who is always reverent, but he who hardens his heart will fall into calamity."

These verses provide a three-step strategy for getting free of our secrets. Think of one secret you are keeping and, as you read about those steps, imagine what it would be like to apply these verses to that specific secret.

1. EXPECT THINGS TO BE TWISTED: HE WHO CONCEALS HIS SIN WILL NOT PROSPER.

Secrets grow in the dark. They have a way of getting stronger the longer they are hidden. Secrets also speak. They convince you that hiding is the best option, so you work to keep your secret out of sight. While you are pouring all your energy into not being found out, you fail to see that other areas of your life are getting twisted.

That's because there are consequences to having a secret:

> Secrets get stronger the longer they are hidden. **>**

* Your *thinking* gets twisted. You fool yourself into believing that you are smart enough to manage the secret and, often, that the best way to handle your deceit is to add more deceit.

* Your *relationships* get twisted. As long as you carry a secret, you'll never be able to fully open up to anyone. Because you aren't able to be yourself with others, you don't let yourself be known by other people. Your secret keeps you from both giving and receiving real love.

* Your *relationship with God* gets twisted. You find it difficult to open up to Him. Whenever you pray, read, or worship, you feel that something is standing between you and God. Fear, insecurity, and pride have driven a wedge between you and God. You always have the feeling that He's displeased with you. Your decision to conceal has complicated everything, but it doesn't have to stay that way. You don't have to cover up.

2. EXPOSE THE TROUBLE: WHOEVER CONFESSES AND FORSAKES . . .

The act of confessing means "to agree with." Your secret has separated you from God; you have been living in conflict with Him and His ways. When you confess your secret, though, you agree that what you've been hiding is against God and therefore is a sin (abuse doesn't fall under this category). You're agreeing with God that what you've been doing in secret is sinful and destructive, that it interferes with His work in your life. Once you confess, the next step is to forsake making up excuses and blaming your choices on others. You assume responsibility for your secret.

Here are some signs a full and open confession needs to be made. You are

* Lying to cover up past and present behavior
* Falsely misrepresenting yourself in a relationship
* Aware that your primary relationships are suffering
* Covering up a secret so you can continue to live in secret
* Involved in destructive behavior
* Escalating your negative behavior(s)
* Unable to quit the secret behavior on your own

If you are doing any of these, it's time to confess your secret. Why is confession necessary? Because—as we've seen—your secret is standing between you and God. And because living in freedom is better than being afraid. Confession cracks—if not totally shatters—the darkness, and whatever you confront in the light, you can conquer. "But if I tell anyone, the truth will tear my life apart!" That's your secret talking to you. Confession will connect you to the compassion of God. When you open up, you will find God stepping in and releasing you from guilt, shame, pressure, and all the emotional stress your secrets have caused. You can be free and you can stay free when you . . .

3. EXIT THE TEMPTATION: HAPPY IS THE MAN WHO IS ALWAYS REVERENT.

Another version reads, "How blessed is the man who fears always" (NASB). In this context the word *fears* is a verb that means "to be prepared and able to resist the temptation of your secret." Now look at that word *FEARS*: each letter suggests an action step for short-circuiting your secrets.

Find a spiritual ally. Don't try to fight your battle alone. Find someone you can be totally truthful with about your struggle, someone you know won't condemn you.

Eliminate everything that fuels your secret. Stay away from places where you might give in to temptation. Block sites. Break off toxic relationships. Clean out the emotional and mental clutter. Doing so will simplify your life.

Apply God's Word. Feeding your mind with Scripture will give you the truth you need to face, fight, and overcome your toxic secrets. Here are some passages you might want to download into your mind: Psalm 32:5; James 4:7; and 1 Timothy 6:11.

Remember that the Spirit of God lives in you. Reminding yourself of this truth will give you courage to live confidently and in the light every moment of every day.

Stand strong. You are not alone. God fights for you. So live each day with perfect confidence that things are right between you and God.

Today, give God your secrets.

#body

Rolling with the Changes *for Guys*

> **GREG CLYDESDALE**
> First Baptist Church, Bossier City, LA

Puberty. I'm pretty sure you've heard that word—but maybe you've asked yourself, *What is it? When is it going to happen? Am I doing it right?* Questions like these go through your mind when you hit your early teenage years. *Puberty* basically means "change." You are changing from a boy to a man, and all change takes time. As your body begins to change and develop, your voice will start to squeak and then get deeper, and you'll notice hair growing all over your body. Growing from a boy to a man means a lot of changes, including taking responsibility for your body. And hygiene is how we take care of our bodies to keep them clean.

Here are a few things you need to know for puberty.

* Deodorant is like sunscreen. You can never put on enough—and reapply, reapply, reapply.
* Take care of your teeth and always carry breath mints with you.
* Shaving is a part of life; learn to enjoy it.
* Pimple cream works.
* Brush your hair; it makes you more respectable.
* You are not always right; sometimes your parents are right.
* God doesn't make junk. He makes all things beautiful (handsome or good-looking, if you prefer)—and that includes you.

Your body change is normal, natural, and even good for you—although at some points you may not agree. Some of the changes—that occasional crack in your voice and those little red dots that pop up on your face—may make you feel a little embarrassed. But you will enjoy other changes, like getting taller, more muscular, and even hairy. All this is part of God's plan.

Yet that doesn't necessarily mean this stage will be easy. I still have nightmares about being in seventh grade. Everyone else

Your body change is normal and natural. >

seemed to be changing much faster than I was! All the boys—and even the girls—were much taller, and the boys in the locker room kept telling me that I stunk. I knew there was no way I could stink. Hey, I took a shower every day. Then . . . it happened! My life-changing moment! The seventh-grade "mean girls" who usually snickered behind my back decided it was time to confront me. Although their actions seemed plenty mean at the time, it was probably the nicest thing those girls could have done. They taught me about deodorant and the equivalent of today's body spray. I didn't know how bad a guy going through puberty could smell—but unfortunately everyone around me knew firsthand.

I hope you don't have to go through a painful life-changing moment like that and will learn right now instead. Here's something else that's good to learn. In 1 Thessalonians 4, Paul wrote about how we can live a life that pleases God. Among the instructions are to avoid sexual immorality and acting on passionate lusts. Verse 4 sums it up by saying that "each of you will control his own body and live in holiness and honor" (NLT). This may not seem terribly relevant to you right now, but as you go through this period of change, your sexual hormones will begin to rage. So remember that one of your jobs as a Christian is to be able to control your bodies, smells and all.

And 1 Corinthians 6:18–20 explains why that job is so important: your body is a temple of the Holy Spirit, so you are to honor God with your body. Think about it. If you knew that God was going to be an overnight guest at your house and spend the night in your room, you'd probably spend a lot of time making sure your room was clean. You'd make the bed, vacuum the floor, and use an air freshener to make the room smell not so gross. Why? Because you knew that the God of the universe would be spending time in that room. You need to do the same for your body that you would do for your bedroom. Keeping your body clean, eating right, exercising, and getting enough sleep are all part of taking care of the temple where the Holy Spirit dwells.

> Keeping your body clean, eating right, exercising, and getting enough sleep are all part of taking care of the temple where the Holy Spirit dwells. **>**

One more word from 1 Corinthians. Paul described the end result of puberty this way: "When I was a child, I spoke as a child, I understood as a child, I thought as a child; but when I became a man, I put away childish things" (13:11). You can and you will get through puberty. In the meantime, try to keep in mind that this is a great time to learn, grow, and see what God has in store for you. Scripture clearly states that even Jesus "grew in wisdom and in stature" (Luke 2:52 NLT). Your brain and your body are growing in such a way that even your view of God will be growing and becoming more mature. God changes from being distant, far away in outer space and living somewhere in heaven. He becomes a God who is intimate and personal.

As you navigate through this time of life, you'll sometimes feel like you're on a roller coaster going up and down. Remember this: God is in control of *everything*. And the God who has created the universe and everything in it also made you. He knows you by name (Exodus 33:17), and He knows how many hairs are on your head (Luke 12:7). That same God has planned for you to go through this change, and He will be at your side every step of the way.

Rolling with the
Changes *for Girls*

> **GREG & AMY CLYDESDALE**
> First Baptist Church, Bossier City, LA

irl to woman—where are you on the spectrum? Maybe several months or even years ago, you noticed changes in your body. (After all, *puberty* means "change"!) You are changing from a girl to a woman. That means a new shape to your body, emotions going a bit haywire, and perhaps being taller than most guys you know. Growing from girl to woman means a lot of changes! One of those changes involves hygiene, keeping your body clean. Hair, skin care, body odor, periods, shaving, makeup, healthy eating, exercise—we girls have a lot to manage. Here are a few tips to help:

> *Puberty* means "change"! >

1. Establish a routine.
2. Talk to your mom or research online about good skin-care techniques.
3. Have your mom or an older trusted female teach you how to dress modestly and apply makeup.
4. Go easy on body spray and perfume.
5. The more you know, the better.

First Corinthians 6:18–20 explains why caring for your body so important: your body is a temple of the Holy Spirit, so you are to honor God with your body. If you were going to have someone come over, you would probably clean your room. You'd make your bed, vacuum, and maybe even hang up your clothes. How important that person is would determine how clean your room needs to be, right? Well, the God of this universe has chosen to have His Spirit dwell in your body—and mine. So you need to do the same for your body that you would do for your bedroom. Keeping your body clean, eating right, exercising, and getting enough sleep are all part of taking care of the temple where the Holy Spirit dwells—and there can be no more important Resident.

One more word from 1 Corinthians. Paul described the end result of puberty this way: "When I was a child, I spoke as a child, I understood as a child, I thought as a child; but when I became a man, I put away childish things" (13:11). You can and you will get through puberty. In the meantime, try to keep in mind that this is a great time to learn, grow, and see what God has in store for you. God is preparing you to be a woman who loves Him, serves Him, and glorifies Him.

Along with the physical changes mentioned above come emotional changes. Mood swings, romantic feelings for boys, anxiety, anger, sadness, feeling the need to "fit in"—emotions like these may sometimes feel harder to deal with than the physical changes. I encourage you to let your parents help you with your roller coaster of emotions. They can help you recognize a mood swing and then coach you through it. The alternative is fighting with your parents all the time—and none of you knowing

> That same God has planned for you to go through this change, and He will be at your side every step of the way. >

why you're fighting in the first place! So when you're talking to your mom about "girl stuff," don't be afraid to bring up how she might help with your emotional ups and downs. That brief conversation—and, yes, it will probably be awkward—can help slow the emotional roller coaster. Maybe the ride won't be so rough.

But it will definitely be a ride! The new issues and decisions, the new responsibilities and opportunities that come at this time of life, aren't a walk in the park! So when you encounter sharp turns, unexpected bumps, and moments of free fall, remember this: God is in control of everything. And the God who created the universe and everything in it also made you. He "knitted [you] together in [your] mother's womb," and you are "fearfully and wonderfully made" (Psalm 139:13–14 ESV). He made you with a beauty that was evident before puberty, will remain during puberty, and will continue throughout your years as a woman. That same God has planned for you to go through this change, and He will be at your side every step of the way.

Taking Care of Your Temple

> **JERRY PIPES**
> Jerry Pipes Productions, Lawrenceville, GA

You are a special person of great worth, created in the very image of God for His special plan and purpose. I love what Zig Ziglar says about you: "You were born to win, engineered for success, and are endowed with seeds of greatness."[1] God's Word, the Bible, puts it this way: "Do you not know that you are God's temple and that God's Spirit dwells in you?" (1 Corinthians 3:16 RSV). What an amazing truth! Your body is the place where the God of the universe dwells through His Holy Spirit. You therefore have a huge privilege and responsibility to take care of your temple, physically, mentally, emotionally, socially, and spiritually. Read God's warning for those who don't take good care of what God has entrusted to us: "If any one destroys God's temple, God will destroy him. For God's temple is holy and that temple you are" (1 Corinthians 3:17 RSV). Sounds serious, doesn't it? It is, so here's a plan for successfully taking care of your temple.

PHYSICAL: DEVELOP AND MAINTAIN A HEALTHY BODY

You've heard it before: eat a healthy diet and exercise three or four times a week. A good physical workout should include:

* Endurance: Do aerobic exercises (biking, swimming, walking, jogging) to get your heart rate up and keep it up for thirty minutes, three or four times per week.
* Flexibility: Stretch before and after aerobic exercise.
* Strength: Tone through calisthenics or weights.

Before beginning a diet and exercise regimen, see your doctor and get a physical to make sure there are no health issues that would make the above suggestions dangerous for you. Also, ask your doctor to help you determine a healthy weight for you. Our society glorifies a too-thin body, so we need objective medical advice. After all, setting an unrealistic weight goal will result in frustration, failure, and potentially an eating disorder. The physical benefits of eating right and exercising regularly are good, but the greatest benefits are emotional: stress is reduced, and self-esteem is enhanced.

MENTAL/EMOTIONAL: DESIGN A PERSONAL GROWTH PLAN

If you want to change any aspect of your behavior, start by changing the way you think. The Bible says, "Do not be conformed to this world but be transformed by the renewal of your mind" (Romans 12:2 RSV). The problem is most people stop learning and growing after their formal education ends. Why? Two primary reasons exist: laziness and television. In most homes, the television is on forty to forty-five hours each week. It imperceptibly shapes our values—and it's addictive. (If you don't think so, just try to do without it for thirty days!) Ask yourself this question: *How do I use this powerful medium to serve my values, accomplish my purpose, and help me grow to my maximum potential?* After you deal with the television issue, develop and implement a personal growth plan. This is one of the most important projects you will ever tackle! Only if you deliberately choose the books you read, the places you go, the experiences you have, and the close friendships you develop will you be more the person you want to be ten, twenty, and thirty years from now.

Consider these suggestions as you start to design a personal growth plan:

* Read great books. If you choose not to read, you are no better off than one who can't read. Not reading is like choosing a self-imposed illiteracy. So, if you have not been reading, begin with a goal of a book a month. An occasional novel is fine, but read great biographies as well.
* Listen to talks, audiobooks, and pod casts while you're in the car and working out.

* Attend conferences.
* Get all you can out of your education.
* Engage in problem solving and planning.
* Laugh every day. Look for the humor in life.

SOCIAL: CHOOSE A POSITIVE ENVIRONMENT

Give me fifteen minutes with your closest friends, and I will be able to tell much about where you're headed in life. That's because people we spend a lot of time with have a huge impact on our lives—on the way we think, feel, act, and react. Does your environment support your values and your efforts to reach your goals? Do the people you spend time with and the places you go help or hinder your efforts to fulfill your dreams?

SPIRITUAL: LET GOD LEAD

It is not enough to have a relationship with Christ; you must spend time developing that relationship. As Paul said, "We are to grow up in every way into him who is the head, into Christ" (Ephesians 4:15 RSV). Paul identified the goal of our growth in this vital relationship as "the measure of the stature of the fulness of Christ" (Ephesians 4:13 RSV). As you develop your relationship with Christ, you will be strengthening your character, clarifying your core values, and making critical decisions concerning your worldview and purpose in life. Here are a few suggestions to consider:

> **Develop your relationship with Christ. >**

* Start every day alone with God: pray and read the Bible.
* Personalize God's Word: read it every day, take good notes when you hear it taught, memorize a verse a week, and meditate on it always.
* Cultivate a powerful prayer life.

* Surround yourself with great friends who will support and sharpen your faith.
* Ask God for daily opportunities to share with others your faith in Christ.
* Decide what you want to accomplish in life and write out a personal mission statement.
* Develop goals based on your mission statement as well as strategies to reach them.

Dear God, I praise You for making me one of a kind. Help me have a soft heart toward You and a real awareness of Your leadership so I can accomplish Your plan and Your purpose for me today.

To Drink or Not to Drink?

DEREK SIMPSON
First Baptist Church Cleveland, Cleveland, TN

irst, some facts.

The use of alcohol by students before the age of twenty-one is illegal. Don't overlook this point! Also, remember that God ordains all authority figures (parents, pastors, teachers, coaches, employers, police, etc.) and that to honor and obey these earthly authorities is to honor and obey our heavenly Authority. To resist earthly authority is to resist God and to invite judgment (Romans 13:2). For some people, the desire to avoid God's "wrath" (Romans 13:4) is motivation enough to not break the law, but Paul offers another reason: your conscience (Romans 13:5). Drinking before the age of twenty-one hardens your heart toward the government's authority to regulate any aspect of your life. If you choose to disobey God's provisional authority relating to alcohol, what will keep you from shoplifting, evading taxes, or vandalizing property? Don't be quick to overlook the restrictions that governing authorities place on alcohol: those rules are not only the government's; they are God's.

God's Word is the ultimate authority for how Christ followers are to live. You must obey the laws of the government because they are ordained by God, but you shouldn't necessarily do everything the laws allow. (Read that sentence again!) Why? Because not every behavior the law allows is helpful or even permitted for a Christ follower. In fact, several behaviors today are forbidden by Scripture but not by the law. (Abortion and gay marriage are two.) So while it's important to obey the laws of the land, it is far more important to remember that Scripture is the ultimate authority and guide for your behavior.

Drunkenness is always a sin. First Corinthians 6:9–10 lists drunkenness with such sinful behaviors as idol worship, adultery, prostitution, homosexuality, thievery, greed, abuse, and cheating. (Clearly, Scripture takes drunkenness far more seriously than our culture does!) All these activities were licensed by the fleshly desires of the old self, but they are utterly inappropriate for those who have been "justified in the name of the Lord Jesus and by the Spirit of our God" (1 Corinthians 6:11). Furthermore, consistent involvement in any of these sinful activities means that the fruit of the Spirit—love, joy, peace, patience, kindness, goodness, faithfulness, gentleness, self-control (Galatians 5:22–23)—will not be as evident in your life.

Alcohol can be very destructive. Although the actual statistics vary from year to year, alcohol is always a factor in the three leading causes of death among fifteen- to twenty-four-year-olds: accidents, homicides, and suicides. Teenagers who use alcohol are also up to seven times more likely to engage in premarital sex, and alcohol may be a factor in up to two-thirds of the reported cases of sexual assault and date rape among high school and college students. Approximately one person in nine who takes that first drink will become an alcoholic. Alcohol-induced liver disease kills approximately twenty thousand people each year, and in 2006, alcohol abuse cost America more than $224 billion.[1] Alcohol hurts family relationships as well: anywhere from 50 to 85 percent of domestic abuse cases involve alcohol.

When it comes to alcohol (and a few similar issues), most students inevitably want to know two things: "Is it right or wrong for me to do it?" and "Do you drink?"

As we've already seen, for students under twenty-one, drinking is always wrong. But for those twenty-one and older, the question must change from "Is it right?" to "Is it wise?"

You've probably already guessed that even though I'm over the age of twenty-one and don't believe the Bible expressly prohibits me from drinking, I choose to abstain from drinking alcohol for several reasons. These are the top two:

1. Drinking could cause me to sin. According to Jeremiah 17:9, my heart is wicked—and so is yours. I have a great enough capacity to sin without introducing addictive substances that could potentially alter my decision making and personality and lead to greater sin, if not total enslavement to alcohol. It's possible that I would not be enslaved by alcohol if I chose to drink socially, but it is absolutely certain that I will not if I abstain.

2. Drinking could cause me to cause others to sin. Paul addressed a real-life example of this: Was it sinful for Christians to eat meat that had been offered to idols? The apostle declared that there is nothing inherently wrong or forbidden about the meat itself, but that because the meat was associated with idol worship and could "wound [the] conscience" of weaker brothers and sisters, he would "never again eat meat, lest I make my brother stumble" (1 Corinthians 8:12–13). To do so, he said, is to sin against fellow believers and to sin against Christ (v. 12).

Let me clarify: it is not always a sin to take a drink, but it is always good to avoid sin, encourage other believers, and protect and preserve your Christian witness.

The Bible on . . . Alcohol

- Genesis 27:28
- Leviticus 10:8–11
- Proverbs 20:1; 21:17; 23:29–35; 31:4–7
- Habakkuk 2:15
- John 2:1–11
- 1 Corinthians 6:10
- Galatians 5:21
- Ephesians 5:18
- 1 Timothy 3:3, 8 >

#faith

Not Just on Sunday

JOSEPH MCMURRY
Carmel Baptist Church, Matthews, NC

This fifteen-year-old boy sat in my office by order of his parents. Jimmy had been suspended from school for breaking the code of conduct, and his parents decided he would not return. As I talked with Jimmy, who was raised in the church by a Christian family, I learned a lot. Basically, Jimmy feels like he has to be a different person depending on where he is and whom he's with. He wasn't claiming to have a split personality; he was telling me that, in order to survive (meaning "be accepted"), he feels as though he has to change according to whomever is around.

* At school, Jimmy is a relatively compliant student. He has no desire to excel in his studies, but he tries not to give his teachers much trouble. Secretly, he thinks that every one of them is an idiot and there is nothing they can tell him that he doesn't already know. He believes he can smile and charm them—and get away with slacking off.

* With his peers at school, Jimmy says inappropriate things and disobeys the rules in order to receive attention. He wants desperately to be cool and will do just about anything to accomplish that.

* Jimmy told me that at church he has to be a "good kid" in order to fit in with the other "good kids." He knows what to say in order to blend in, and he can answer any question in Sunday school. Jimmy gives his leaders and teachers absolutely no reason to suspect that his life is any different when he leaves the church building.

* In his neighborhood, however, Jimmy becomes a very different person in order to fit in. He enjoys the activities the neighborhood kids participate in and wants to be a part of their crowd, so he uses language he knows his parents and church leaders would disapprove of. He participates

  • • • • • • • • • • • • • • • • •

in activities that are vandalistic, unhealthy, and illegal, including the destruction of property and experimenting with drugs and alcohol. As long as no one from any other segment of his life is around, he doesn't care if his language is offensive or if his behavior is destructive.

* At home, Jimmy follows the rules and behaves himself as much as he feels is necessary in order to stay in his parents' good graces. Just like at school, he manipulates his parents in order for things to go his way. When he talks to his parents about life outside the home, he tells them that everyone is against him, none of the students at school like him, and all of the teachers hate him even though he never does anything wrong. Jimmy also tells his parents that the people at church are judgmental, and they wouldn't care if he didn't ever come back. Of course, his stories are not true, but his parents—who love him—have no reason to doubt what he says.

Does this real-life example seem too extreme? Or does Jimmy's life remind you too much of your own life? Living a compartmentalized life is a reality for many young people (and adults, for that matter), even for those young people who claim to be Christians. (In fact, I would even argue that compartmentalization is more likely to occur in students from Christian homes than in students whose families have no religious affiliation, but that's a topic for another day.)

We compartmentalize when we create sections in our lives and believe that what happens in one section has no effect on other sections. We find comfort, for instance, in being able to put sins in one compartment, either ignoring or being unaware that the consequences of our sin will impact every other dimension of our lives.

> **Segmenting our lives leads to lukewarm Christianity. >**

Segmenting our lives leads to, among other things, lukewarm Christianity.

Jesus told us, "I know your deeds, that you are neither cold nor hot. I wish you were either one or the other! So, because you are lukewarm—neither hot nor cold—I am about to spit you out of my mouth" (Revelation 3:15–16 NIV). Jesus also taught that if we separate our lives into compartments apart from the Spirit, then we have misunderstood what it means to live in relationship with Him (Matthew 7:21–23).

Compartmentalizing is like pouring a pitcher of water into several different glasses. Obviously the water from the pitcher has been separated from its original container. God does not want us to compartmentalize the different aspects of our lives; He wants our relationship with Him to transform every area of our life.

Continuing the water analogy, if a drop of food coloring is added to the pitcher of water, it changes the color of all the water in the pitcher. God's intention is that His presence in our lives would in the same way change our total existence and His love would permeate every aspect of our lives.[1] That kind of total transformation can't happen if, so to speak, the water has been poured into several glasses.

Maybe you can relate to Jimmy. And maybe you're finding it exhausting to be a different person in each setting you find yourself. Are you worried about being judged—and is that keeping you from talking to someone the way Jimmy talked with me? From gaining a better understanding of the joy that comes only from having a right relationship with God and living in light of His love?

You won't fall in love with Jesus by just showing up at church once a week. So give yourself a chance to know Jesus better. Spend time with someone in whom you see the benefits of living a unified rather than a compartmentalized life.

How Do I Get Back?

KELLY KNOUSE
Idlewild Baptist Church, Lutz, FL

I clearly remember the red cap and gown I wore and the way the evening unfolded. After all, it was a very significant milestone in my life: high school graduation. Maybe you've already passed that milestone, and if you have, I'm guessing it was pretty similar to mine. The real excitement of the big event begins near the end of the ceremony, when the principal announces to the parents and guests, "Ladies and gentlemen, I present to you the graduating class of twenty-whatever! Graduates, you may move your tassels!" Then the excitement explodes. Everyone throws their caps in the air. Girls cry, the guys high-five, and then everyone says something really deep to each other like, "I'll never forget you," or, "We'll always be friends," or, "Stay in touch."

Now fast-forward ten years. You open your high school yearbook and say, "Oh, I'd totally forgotten about so-and-so, the guy I said I'd *always* be friends with!" What happened? I'll tell you what happened: the fellowship changed.

The apostle John knew about fellowship that changes. That's why he explained that when we receive Jesus Christ, there is something that can never change and something that can change. What cannot change is *relationship*. Once we become a son or daughter of God, we are always His son or daughter. That is an unchanging relationship. However, what can change is *fellowship*. We can become distant. We find ourselves in a place where we don't talk anymore, don't hang out anymore. What has changed is our fellowship with the Lord. And that change, according to John, is caused by one thing: sin.

So how do we come back? How do we restore fellowship that is broken? John listed three steps.

First, we must *specifically identify our sins*: "If we say that we have no sin, we deceive ourselves" (1 John 1:8). We must first admit to ourselves that we have sinned. We need to call our sins what they are—sin! We didn't just make a mistake; it wasn't just an oversight. God forgives sins, not alibis or excuses. When we sin, we offend the heart of God. In any relationship that is strained by an offense, we must specifically address the wound we caused. It's one thing to admit to ourselves that we have sinned, but that's only the first step.

Second, we must *confess our sins immediately*. It's not enough to acknowledge our sins in our own heart and mind. After we admit our sins to ourselves, then each one of us has to say, "Lord, I have sinned." We have to name our sins and nail them to the cross: "Lord, I not only admit I have sinned, but I confess that sin." And what response does God promise in His Word? "If we confess our sins, He is faithful and just to forgive us our sins and to cleanse us from all unrighteousness" (1 John 1:9). One of the biggest cancers in the Christian life is unconfessed sin. The longer a sin lingers, the more damage it causes and the more distant the relationship becomes. Because we're human beings, confessing our sins immediately pretty much means confessing our sins continually, but we can do that confidently. We can be absolutely sure that God forgives us every time we sin and confess to Him that sin.

> **3 STEPS:**
>
> 1. Identify your sin.
> 2. Confess your sin.
> 3. Turn from your sin. **>**

There's one more thing to do to get back into fellowship with God. We need to *completely turn from our sins*. Turning from sin must be a twofold process. First, we must turn our backs to sin: at a specific moment we choose to change the behavior that led to the broken fellowship in the first place. Second, we must turn our hearts to God and be open to receiving His forgiveness—that's where Jesus Christ comes in.

First John 2:1 says, "If anyone sins, we have an Advocate with the Father, Jesus Christ the righteous." That word *advocate* is a fancy word that means "lawyer." The prosecuting attorney is the devil, who accuses and condemns us day and night before God's throne. He says to the Judge, "Your Honor, this is Kelly Knouse, and he is a sinner." He names my sins (something I'm not going to do for you, thank you very much). And he's right about every single item . . . and I am so ashamed.

> Turning from sin is a twofold process:
>
> 1. Turn from sin.
>
> 2. Turn your heart to God. **>**

Then my Advocate, the Lord Jesus Christ, steps forward and requests permission to approach the bench. Think about that! What a great moment when your Attorney approaches the bench and says, "Hey, Dad!" The Lord Jesus, our Advocate, our Lawyer, says, "Everything the prosecutor said is right, but I bear on My hands the marks of payment for Kelly's sins. I forgave him. And, Father, You said that everyone whose sins I have covered would be right with You and with this Court."

Then the Judge will say, "Would the accused please stand? This is your sentence. There is 'no condemnation to [you] who are in Christ Jesus, who do not walk according to the flesh, but according to the Spirit' (Romans 8:1)."

And you know what? I'm back in! I'm back in fellowship with God, back talking to Him again, back hanging out with Him, back on the path to intimacy with Him. All is well because I identified, confessed, and turned from my sin. I admitted my sin to myself, I agreed with God about its sinfulness, and I relied on my Advocate to provide all that was necessary for my renewed fellowship with God. He is your Advocate too.

Guilt or Grace?

JODY GAMBRELL
First Baptist Church of Pensacola, Pensacola, FL

I believe I owe you an apology. As an ordained minister of the gospel and an employee of a local church, I make this apology on behalf of churches across America that are selling a guilt-laced gospel. Let me try to explain—but since I haven't received permission from those churches, please don't mention this article to them.

I became a Christian during my early teenage years. The gospel was preached, the Holy Spirit moved, the invitation was given, I walked down the aisle, I prayed with my pastor, I filled out a membership card, and—boom!—no hell for this guy. I was *saved*! I had witnessed many of my friends getting saved according to this same magic formula. And I believed that the gospel was what I had to believe in order to be saved. I remember thinking, *I am a Christian. Now what?*

I grew up going to church every Sunday. I had been around Christians all my life. I knew how they acted and what they looked like. I had heard hundreds of sermons from dozens of preachers. With all this church experience, I was pretty sure I knew how to do this Christian thing. I was taught to love God, do good things, and don't do bad things. (I could have missed some deeper theological sermon points while playing tic-tac-toe and MASH during church.)

I wanted to be the best Christian I could be. If God were going to choose a Christian all-star team, I wanted to be chosen first. I started working hard to earn God's favor. I got busy for God! I attempted to rid all sin from my life (LOL). I read my Bible daily. I tried not to fall asleep during my nightly prayers. I started a prayer journal. I became extremely active in my youth group. I joined the youth choir. I helped old ladies cross the street. I carried my Bible to school. I tithed my minimum-wage (plus tips) paycheck that I earned from sacking groceries at the local supermarket. I would've even joined Acteens if they'd allowed boys to join. (Still bitter.) I had mastered the items on my spiritual "to do" list and was doing a pretty good job of avoiding the major sins too.

But being a Christian turned out to be exhausting! I was constantly wondering if God was even noticing my efforts to make His all-star team. "Hey, God! Do You see me down here? . . . Aren't You proud of me? . . . Am I doing a good job?" After I had a few months of an all-star-caliber performance under my belt, fatigue set in, and I started making costly errors. *Is my position on the team in jeopardy?* I wondered. I also started noticing other Christians who seemed to be better spiritual athletes than I was, and I became extremely jealous of them. My desire to please God was making me resent Him and His high, hard-to-reach standards. Just as Martin Luther noted, my fear of God's judgment was producing a hatred for Him that was driving my heart further and further away from Him. On the surface, my actions probably looked godly enough, but inside I had begun to worry about being cut from the team.

I was very aware that my efforts never quite measured up. I knew that, even on my best day, my performance was not good enough to earn a spot. And that's not just true for me. The Bible teaches us that our righteous acts are like "filthy rags" or, in my metaphor, a sweaty jersey (Isaiah 64:6). That means all the "super Christians" I'd once been jealous of didn't perform well enough to make the cut either. In fact, the Bible tells us that no one is good enough to make the team (Romans 3:10). Well, no one—except for the Coach's Son.

Our best efforts to live a godly life result in sweat-stained jerseys, but there is One whose jersey is covered

> Our spot in God's kingdom has absolutely *nothing* to do with our performance and *everything* to do with Christ's performance. **>**

in blood. His name is Jesus, and it was His flawless performance that secured my spot on the team. The Bible tells us that God "made [Jesus] who knew no sin to be sin for us, that we might become the righteousness of God in Him" (2 Corinthians 5:21). *This* is the gospel. Our spot in God's kingdom has absolutely *nothing* to do with our performance and *everything* to do with Christ's performance. He took my sins—and yours—to the cross and died so that we could make the team. At the cross Jesus exchanged our sins for His righteousness. "How is this fair?" you ask. It isn't fair; it's *grace*. This is good news!

> The gospel isn't simply the power of God to *save* us; it's the power of God to *change* us once we're saved. **>**

As a young teenager, I believed that the gospel was simply what I needed to believe in order to be saved. I did not realize that the gospel isn't simply the power of God to *save* us; it's the power of God to *change* us once we're saved. The gospel is not simply our ticket into heaven, but it's also God's power to sanctify us as we grow as His children. Jesus is the basis of our salvation. It has *nothing* to do with us. We bring nothing to the table.

So if you are a Christian, you are free. Paul said, "For freedom Christ has set us free" (Galatians 5:1 ESV). You are free from the guilt that comes with trying to make the team when your efforts aren't good enough—and never will be. So please accept my apology if you've been sold a guilt-laced gospel. You are free because Jesus paid the price for all your sins. Accept His free gift of grace and start living in the freedom that you can only find in Jesus.

Advantage Us!

JODY GAMBRELL
First Baptist Church of Pensacola, Pensacola, FL

Have you ever wondered what it must have been like to be a disciple? And not just any disciple, but one of *the* disciples. One of the original Twelve. (Or at least original *Eleven*. Not many people want to be Judas.) Imagine having Jesus Himself invite you to be a follower . . . and then walking with Him every day? How might you have reacted when you finally realized that this Rabbi really was the Son of God? What would you have thought the first time you saw Him heal someone? How cool to have witnessed Jesus take a kid's fish stick Lunchable and turn it into a meal that fed thousands! How freaked out would you have been when Jesus walked on water toward your boat? Imagine the devastating sorrow and indescribable pain at seeing the Man you loved falsely accused and brutally executed. And then came confusion and fear . . . followed three days later by that unforgettable moment when you were reunited with the risen Jesus! Being in that inner circle would have been really cool.

It's easy to think that the original disciples had an advantage over modern-day disciples. They walked with Jesus instead of just reading about Him in the Bible. They had face-to-face conversations with Him instead of just praying. You and I read about Jesus' teachings, but the disciples had Him as their personal Trainer. Wouldn't you think that, with Jesus at their side, the disciples could not fail?

Despite having direct access to Jesus Himself, the disciples were constantly messing up. Like us modern-day followers of Christ, the disciples were flawed. They were impulsive, boisterous, pessimistic, selfish, intolerant, devious, materialistic—and they were slow learners. Yet Jesus chose these flawed men to be His ambassadors to the world. And because they were human, I'm sure that this opportunity was a source of pride for the disciples. After all, *they* were in the Son of God's entourage! But then membership in that select group got more difficult.

In John 16, Jesus told His disciples that He would soon leave them. "What! You can't be serious Jesus!" Scripture tells us the disciples were full of sorrow (John 16:6). Their lives had been totally changed by this Man—and now He was leaving them. But Jesus had more to say: "It is to your advantage that I go away; for if I do not go away, the Helper will not come to you; but if I depart, I will send Him to you" (John 16:7). Who was this "Helper"? This Helper is the Holy Spirit, whom Jesus earlier had promised to send: "I will ask the Father, and he will give you another Helper, to be with you forever" (John 14:16 ESV). Jesus also told His disciples that they would do even greater things than He had done (John 14:12)—and these very ordinary men had seen Jesus do some pretty miraculous things. I'm thinking Thomas wasn't the only disciple doubting Jesus at this point!

After His death and resurrection, the disciples spent forty more days with Jesus. But would these men be able to accomplish their mission without Jesus at their side? Jesus spoke to that concern right before He left the earth. Reminding His disciples of His earlier promise, He told them, "You shall receive power when the Holy Spirit has come upon you; and you shall be witnesses to Me in Jerusalem, in all Judea and Samaria, and to the end of the earth" (Acts 1:8). And these are Jesus' last recorded words. The Man whom the disciples had devoted their lives to "was taken up, and a cloud received Him out of their sight" (Acts 1:9). Their mission was clearly defined, but without Jesus to lead, how would these ordinary men carry out that mission?

Undoubtedly, had they had to rely on their own power, the disciples would have failed miserably. But Jesus had promised a Helper, and Jesus was true to His word. In Acts 2, the Helper entered the scene, and the disciples were forever changed. The fisherman Peter, for instance, preached at Pentecost, and three thousand people were saved (Acts 2:41). The disciples immediately recognized the power of the Holy Spirit. Jesus' promise of the Helper had indeed become a reality. These average Joes would go on to change the world.

I've come to realize that Jesus' original disciples did not have an advantage over us who follow Him today. In fact—as Jesus taught—*we* actually have the advantage because His Holy Spirit literally dwells within us: "the Spirit of Him who raised Jesus from the dead dwells in you" (Romans 8:11). We put Jesus' disciples on a pedestal, but we have the very same Helper that Jesus' disciples had. The Spirit within us gives us the ability to fly, but too often we continue to be satisfied walking.

Many of us Christians try our best to follow Christ by relying on our own strength and abilities. But just like the original disciples, we are flawed, so our best efforts to follow Jesus in our own power will never be quite good enough. So let's rely on the Helper God has given us, on His Spirit who "dwells with you and will be in you" (John 14:17). We must submit to the leadership and guidance of the Holy Spirit: He will direct our paths, He is helping us to become more holy, and He is always interceding on our behalf. In all that we do, then, we must choose to rely not on our own strength but on the power of our great Helper, the Holy Spirit of God.

> The Spirit within us gives us the ability to fly, but too often we continue to be satisfied walking. **>**

The disciples changed the world after they submitted to the Holy Spirit's leadership. And I don't know if you've heard the news, but Jesus' original twelve disciples are no longer with us. That means it's our turn—yours and mine—to change the world. Know that the Spirit is with you!

Tending to Your Personal Environment

ROGER GLIDEWELL
Global Youth Ministry, Chatsworth, GA

You're heard the news: The atmosphere is warming. The oceans are rising. The ice cap is shrinking. The bad news about our environment can be overwhelming. If all the prognostications about earth's demise are true, what can we do about it?

Well, we can and we should do something. Genesis 1:28 reminds us that God Himself made us responsible for His creation. Even people who have no regard for God have attempted to address environmental concerns. They're behind the efforts to save trees, recycle, drive energy-efficient cars, make sure factories don't pollute—the list goes on.

A REASON THAT MATTERS

While all of these admonitions provide good reason to cooperate, there is still a better motivation than whatever campaigns, demonstrations, and government mandates come up with, and it's this: As believers we take action to clean up our environment because we want to. And we want to in order to bring glory to our God, who created it all.

When you and I were restored to our Creator through faith in Christ, He—in the form of His Holy Spirit—took up residence within us (1 Corinthians 6:19–20). Hebrews 9:14 says Jesus moved in and cleaned house. His first act was to "cleanse [our] conscience." That's why I consider Jesus the Ultimate Environmentalist. You see, environmentalism isn't just about Mother Nature; it's about God's nature, about His holiness. Since all creation is a reflection of God, restoring creation is Jesus' priority—and it is to be our priority too!

We believers should be God's walking advertisements for purity, "the fragrance of Christ among those who are being saved and among those who are perishing" (2 Corinthians 2:15). God desires to restore all His creation—not only the world but also everyone in it—to its original pristine condition. So what should you and I do about our personal environment, both internal and external? Here are three simple steps to take:

STEP # 1: TAKE OUT THE TRASH IN MY HEART

We can't let clutter accumulate in or around our lives. Sin is an inner attitude before it is an outward act. In 1 John 1:9, the apostle wrote, "If we confess our sins, he is faithful and just to forgive us our sins and to cleanse us from all unrighteousness." We need to get rid of sin quickly before it smells! We should also clean up our unkempt personal appearance and cluttered personal space, because both mar God's glory. If we don't care about taking these steps, we need to repent. Do you need to check your attitude about ignoring and doing nothing about the clutter in your world that defaces God's creation and dishonors His majesty? Or do you just thoughtlessly walk by the gum wrapper on the hallway floor—or worse, did you throw the gum wrapper there?

Step #1 Prayer: *Lord, help me to see Your world as You see it, as a reflection of Your very nature. Help me stop being part of the problem.*

STEP #2: TAKE CHARGE OF MY PERSONAL SPACE

Start with your own room. And I can hear your response: "Wait! The Bible doesn't say anything about cleaning my room!" No, but it talks about taking responsibility for God's world, and that begins with keeping your own personal space clean. Listen, your mother (or roommate) is right to bug you to clean your room. Mom knows that you must stop depending on others and start taking care of yourself. After all, if you'd never learned to take care of yourself, you'd still be in diapers, depending on others to wipe your bottom for you. Does that sound attractive? I hope not! Taking care of your own personal space is a sign of maturity.

Furthermore, when you keep your space clean, people around you are more likely to respect you. Imagine your mom watching in awe as you roll the vacuum into your room! "It's okay, Mom. Jesus wants me to take care of my space. Hey, is there a hyperdrive on this thing that can suck in the monster dust bunnies under my bed?" When you start caring for the space you call yours, you are demonstrating self-sufficiency, a parent's dream come true. More importantly, you bring honor to your heavenly Father.

Step #2 Prayer: *Lord, give me the determination to get my personal environmental act together.*

STEP # 3: TAKE APPROPRIATE CARE OF ANY SPACE I OCCUPY

Now for a probably unexpected career tip: taking appropriate personal responsibility for whatever space you may occupy—especially when it's clearly not your space to keep clean—will set you up for more rapid advancement in life.

It's true! When you take on the responsibility of improving whatever space you occupy—whether it is clearing the next table's trash at McDonald's or picking up trash in the school parking lot—you are helping others. These small acts of service add value to your employer's workplace, to the neighborhood, to whatever space you are improving.

And don't think your efforts will go unnoticed! You don't believe it? Have you seen how nasty public bathrooms can get? If you work at one of those places, try this: volunteer to clean the bathrooms first thing each time you go to work. (Take a heart pill to your boss when you make this offer!) If you consistently improve your workplace, you *will* get the boss's attention and, as I said, you may advance more rapidly than other employees who rarely go the extra mile—or inch—to improve the workplace.

Step #3 Prayer: *Lord, help me take action to improve whatever space I occupy.*

Yes, Jesus is the Ultimate Environmentalist, and He does this good work through you.

So accept responsibility for whatever space you occupy, even when you don't have to, and you will honor God, bless others, and maybe even get a raise at work.

Forgiveness Brings Freedom

RICK YOUNG
First Baptist Church, Woodstock, GA

Bearing with one another, and forgiving one another, if anyone has a complaint against another; even as Christ forgave you, so you also must do.

—COLOSSIANS 3:13

When we read that instruction to believers, we know that the world and Satan would disagree. "Get even" is their message. If you are wronged, if a friend does something against you, if a family member disappoints you, it is your right to make sure you get back at whoever has done you wrong and come out on top. Even though our sinful nature would love to follow this advice, we can't give in to this temptation.

And one reason is that forgiveness is not about us, and forgiveness is not about getting even. Forgiveness is about bringing glory to God, but we also benefit. If we don't practice forgiveness, bitterness will take root in our hearts and grow. Forgiveness brings joy and happiness. Consider these differences between forgiveness and unforgiveness:

Forgiveness:	Unforgiveness:
Peace	Violence
Healing	Pain
Rest	Unrest
Happiness	Conflict

Admittedly, it is sometimes very difficult to give forgiveness, but God desires and commands that we forgive and that we do so freely. Here are some action steps you can take on the road to forgiveness, even when you find yourself dealing with some of your life's greatest hurts.

Find help with God. It is impossible for us to give forgiveness on our own;

> Forgiveness is about bringing glory to God, but we also benefit. **>**

we need God's help. We human beings, with our sinful nature, want to hold on to anger and bitterness. We do not want to give forgiveness because our anger and hurt tell us that we need to get back at the person who did us wrong. With God's help and our willingness to read, obey, and act on His words, we can find the strength to give forgiveness to others.

Openly admit unforgiveness. The only way we can get free of our unforgiveness is to admit that we are holding on to it and that we need a change of heart. Only when we acknowledge our unforgiveness can we begin the process of forgiveness. Being honest with God and ourselves will help us release our bitterness and give forgiveness.

Remember that you have been forgiven. God has forgiven us Christians for so much. Before we knew Jesus, we were enemies of God because of our sinful ways (Romans 3:23). But the Bible teaches that "God demonstrates His own love toward us, in *that while we were still sinners*, Christ died for us" (Romans 5:8, emphasis added). We also hear God's gracious words through the prophet Jeremiah: "I will forgive their iniquity, and their sin I will remember no more" (31:34). God has been very gracious to us as Christians, so we need to remember everything He has forgiven for us and extend the same forgiveness to others.

Give forgiveness. To truly understand forgiveness and be able to give it, we must understand what forgiveness is *not*. Forgiveness is not a feeling; it is a choice that we can make with God's help. God gives us grace, and we must give such grace to others even when we do not feel like it. Giving the gift of forgiveness will change how we feel about that person and about the situation that calls for forgiveness. We will see the person and the event through God's eyes instead of relying on how we feel. Forgiveness is one of the greatest gifts that we can give even if it is not accepted. Forgiveness will change us and our walk with God.

It must be forgotten. Once we have made the choice to forgive, we next need to forget the problem so we can move on with our lives. Too many times we hold on to something that has been done to us even when we say we have forgiven. We must move on and not keep a history of wrongs done against us. Imagine if God had done that with us. What if He never forgot the long list of things that we've done wrong? I love Psalm 103:12: "As far as the east is from the west, so far has He removed our transgressions [our wrongs] from us." Forgiven by God, we Christians have the great opportunity to move on and forget just as the Lord has done for us.

Vengeance is not part of forgiveness. So many times when someone does something against us, we want to get back at them. We want to make sure that they are paid back for the wrong they did against us, but God would not have us think that way. Vengeance is not ours to give. God spoke clearly that vengeance is His: "Beloved, never avenge yourselves, but leave it to the wrath of God, for it is written, 'Vengeance is mine, I will repay, says the Lord'" (Romans 12:19 ESV). We do not have to worry about getting even. God will take care of justice; our responsibility is to give forgiveness.

> Forgiveness is not a feeling; it is a choice that we can make with God's help. **>**

Establish relationships again. The whole reason to give forgiveness is to enable us to have great relationships with family and friends. We were created to live in community and to be in relationships with other people.

Unforgiveness builds walls between us and others. Without forgiveness, we cannot experience true fellowship, laughter, and love.

Okay, so we understand we are to forgive, but we may have the same question Peter did. We want to know how many times we have to give forgiveness. Peter asked, "Up to seven times?" Jesus said to him, "I do not say to you, up to seven times, but up to seventy times seven" (Matthew 18:21–22).

Unforgiveness is a form of pride that rejects God and that allows Satan to have a portion of our hearts and a foothold in our lives. Forgiveness, however, frees you from the prison of unforgiveness. So start today to give forgiveness, and you'll discover true freedom.

Why Am I Never Content?

BRIAN MANUEL
Maplewood First Baptist Church, Sulpher, LA

How often do you wrestle with the question "Why am I never content?" It seems that we Christians today are no different from people outside the church when it comes to this issue. Apparently all of us are looking for something that will give us a sense of peaceful satisfaction. We often compare our lives to the people around us, and we hear society teach us that a person's value is measured by professional success and net worth. When we don't measure up to those standards, we feel empty and unsettled.

So what does it mean to be content? According to *Webster's, content* means "to be satisfied with what one is or has; not wanting more or anything else." Are you the type of person whose emotions are determined by the circumstances of your life? Or can you honestly say that you lack nothing? Also, why is it that believers who have been given a hope and a future in Jesus Christ don't find fulfillment in Him?

> Are you the type of person whose emotions are determined by the circumstances of your life? >

In 2004, I met Master Sergeant John F. who was serving in the United States Air Force. John was a remarkable man who had not only served his country well but was also a committed husband and father. He took pride in his personal accomplishments, his ability to provide for his family, and what his job had allowed him to acquire. Not surprisingly, this military man lived a regimented life: everything had its place and was to be done in a specific way. On Saturday, August 27, 2005, two days prior to Hurricane Katrina making landfall, I stopped by John's house to check on him and his family before I left town. John told me that he was confident that everything was going to be okay and he wasn't concerned about the storm because he could handle it. He had no idea how different his life would be two days later.

John lost his house and everything he owned, everything he had worked for, the very things he took pride in. At church the following Sunday, September 4, I found myself holding John in my arms as he wept profusely. At that moment in his life, he had no hope, no purpose, and nothing to cling to. And John was not alone: hundreds, if not thousands of people around him also felt hopeless. Why was John without hope? What the apostle Paul wrote in Philippians 4:12 (NLT) may help us answer that question:

> I know how to live on almost nothing or with everything. I have learned the secret of living in every situation, whether it is with a full stomach or empty, with plenty or little.

Paul claimed to have found the "secret" to a life of contentment. He claimed that, regardless of the circumstances of his life, whether they were good or bad, he could be content. How is this possible? For my friend John, *contentment* meant remaining in control of his life, but for Paul control did not determine contentment. In verse 13, Paul shared his secret: "I can do all things through Christ who strengthens me." For years I thought this verse referred to a supernatural ability that we possess because we have a relationship with Christ. But that interpretation couldn't be right if I never felt content. At that time, I was no different from John: I was okay as long as life was okay.

So why was Paul able be content? Philippians 4:6–7 (NLT) says this:

> Don't worry about anything; instead, pray about everything. Tell God what you need, and thank him for all he has done. Then you will experience God's peace,

which exceeds anything we can understand. His peace will guard your hearts and minds as you live in Christ Jesus.

Paul could be content because he did not allow himself to hold on to things he had no control over. His heart was guarded from discontent because what he gave to God he allowed God to keep instead of trying to control it himself. This does not mean that Paul never worried about anything in life; he was saying, though, that he ultimately placed his hope and trust in Christ. Philippians 3:8 (NLT) describes why Paul was able to have this mind-set:

Everything else is worthless when compared with the infinite value of knowing Christ Jesus my Lord. For his sake I have discarded everything else, counting it all as garbage, so that I could gain Christ.

Nothing in Paul's life was of any value to him compared to the infinite value of knowing his Savior. In fact, Paul counted everything as garbage compared to knowing Christ. John, however, valued everything in his life and found significance in what he had acquired, so when he lost it all, he felt a huge void. John had heard the gospel and accepted Jesus as his Savior earlier in life, but he could not comprehend all that his relationship with Christ could be as long as he focused on the temporal things in his life.

So the secret to being content lies in understanding and embracing the sufficiency of Jesus. That sounds simple enough, but we all still struggle to find satisfaction. Why? Each of us finds the answer to that question when we look inward and realize that we value the wrong things.

Jesus should be the champion of your life and mine. It took John losing everything before he embraced the sufficiency of Christ in his life. What will it take for you to do the same?

Gaining an Accurate View of God

JOHN PAUL BASHAM
Liberty Baptist, Hampton, VA

In his book *The Knowledge of the Holy*, A. W. Tozer states, "Wrong ideas about God are not only the fountain from which the polluted waters of idolatry flow; they are themselves idolatrous." Do you see what he said? It is a frightening prospect that even we Christians might be idolaters because we have an incomplete or incorrect view of God. Consider the powerfully convicting truth of Tozer's statement: any view of God that is inconsistent with Scripture is an offense to the Almighty's name.

> Christians might be idolaters because we have an incomplete or incorrect view of God. >

So what view of God does Scripture offer us? Put simply, who *is* God? Far too often we in the church draw on the unfailing and immeasurable love of God, yet we fail to truly and intimately know Him and His character. We encourage unbelievers to accept His love and receive salvation, but we fail to urge them to follow Him toward holiness and, along the way, get to know His character and such amazing traits as His mercy, sovereignty, and justice.

In fact, one of the most crippling issues facing the church today is our inadequate view of God. Whether resulting from life experience, family history, bad teaching, or the complete absence of any biblical education, nearly everyone has a different view of God. If the body of Christ is to be healthy, our understanding of the essence of God's character is a critical foundational truth. None of us—whatever our age, whether we are seminary educated or "just" a faithful worshiper—should neglect the whole counsel of God's Word.

Every believer needs to pursue a solid understanding of the fullness of who God has revealed Himself to be.

In *The Attributes of God*, A. W. Pink wrote, "There are many today who talk about the love of God, who are total strangers to the God of love." Sadly, this statement is true for both believers and unbelievers. One of the most common ways that God is misrepresented in the church is in our single-mindedness regarding the love of God. Although God's love is undeniable in the pages of Scripture (1 John 4:8; Psalm 63:3; Romans 5:8), we must learn to worship Him in His fullness, acknowledging every aspect of His character. We see God's love throughout the Old Testament as He led His people out of Egypt, freed them from the bonds of slavery, appointed leaders for them, and taught them how to live a life that would please Him. In the New Testament, we see more of this same love in the ways Jesus Christ cared for people, trained His disciples for ministry, taught in the synagogues, healed the sick, and offered Himself for the forgiveness of sins. But as we celebrate these acts of *love*, will we overlook God's sovereign *power* on display when He parted the waters of the Red Sea or His justice when He poured out His wrath against sin on the cross of Christ? There is no doubt that God's love for His children is unfailing and unchanging, but we do Him a disservice—we dishonor Him and shortchange ourselves in our relationship with Him—when we do not consider the fullness of His glorious character as it is displayed in Scripture.

When we limit the greatness of God to even His immeasurable love, our view of God falls short of Scripture's revelation of His complete nature. We have to realize that each one of God's attributes is perfectly complemented by the others, making the study of all of His characteristics crucial to developing a true understanding of God. An incomplete view of God is an inaccurate view.

So keeping in mind God's love, consider now His holiness. Wayne Grudem said, "God's holiness means that He is separated from sin and devoted to seeking His own honor." In light of this definition, we can see in a new way the great lengths God went to, to show His love for us. Our holy God—unable by nature to tolerate sin—nevertheless reached out to us sinners in love, through His holy Son Jesus. Paul said it best in Romans: "God demonstrates His own love toward us, in that while we were still sinners, Christ died for us" (5:8).

God seeks His own honor and His own glory in all that He does, but especially in His display of love in the death and resurrection of Christ. God is also worthy of honor and glory because He stands alone in His holiness. And how beautiful are His love and His jealous desire for our joy to be found in Him alone, for He is the only Joy Giver. Dare we separate God's holiness from His love and risk creating a loving God who does not also jealously point us to Himself?

A wise pastor once said, "Your view of God determines everything else." If you fail to see God in the fullness of His glory, neglecting such attributes as His mercy, holiness, wrath, righteousness, and sovereignty, you will fail to know God for who He is . . . and yourself for who you were created to be.

What will you do to get to know the Almighty better?

Christianity—It's Not What You Do; It's Who You Are

BRIAN MANUEL
Maplewood First Baptist Church, Sulpher, LA

I f you were to ask the average nonchurchgoer to describe what Christianity is all about, what do you think you'd hear? Some would probably say that it's a group of delusional people who believe in a fictitious god. Others might say that Christianity is about following a set of rules designed to keep you from having a good time or that it's all about attending church regularly and trying to be a good, moral person. If you were to ask the same question of people who profess to be Christians, I would like to think that the responses would be very different. Sadly, that is not the case, and, in fact, it is very rare that I hear a response that has a biblical foundation. Most often I hear that being a Christian is believing in God and Jesus, trying your best to do what Scripture instructs you to do, regularly attending church—and regularly giving money, loving your family, and treating others kindly. Somewhere in the history of the church, our relationship with Jesus Christ has been reduced to a laundry list of things we do. If that's the case, then what is the difference between Christians and the average person who lives a decent, moral life? Case in point . . .

Several years ago I met a young man named Michael. Of the thousands of people I have encountered during my ministry, he is the most genuine and kindhearted person I have ever met. Michael served at an at-risk teen center, volunteered to mentor kids, and was always willing to help those in need. Over the years, he became a close friend of the family. Initially, many of us assumed that Michael was a Christian based on his moral standards and selflessness. Michael had been raised in the Catholic Church, and by both the world's standards and his own, he was a good person. After countless attempts to have a conversation with him about his personal spiritual life, however, I realized that he didn't have one. The reason? He understood Christianity to be based entirely on his works. He was focused on doing more good than wrong. Michael thought God's favor depended on what he did, not on the person of Jesus Christ, His sacrificial death, and His grace. Ephesians 2:8–9 (NLT) says this:

> God saved you by his grace when you believed. And you can't take credit for this; it is a gift from God. Salvation is not a reward for the good things we have done, so none of us can boast about it.

The apostle Paul clearly pointed out that salvation has nothing to do with our works. Michael wanted God to love him for what he did and in some regards expected God to love him because of his works. When we take what we do out of the equation, then the focus is on Christ and not ourselves. But if what we do doesn't make us a Christian, what does? In Ephesians 1:13 (NLT), Paul wrote this:

> Salvation has nothing to do with our works. >

> Now you Gentiles have also heard the truth, the Good News that God saves you. And when you believed in Christ, he identified you as his own by giving you the Holy Spirit, whom he promised long ago.

Paul identified a believer as someone who had been marked by God as His own and who, as a result, had received the Holy Spirit as a spiritual marker. Being a Christian is not at all about what we do; it is who we are as a result of what Jesus Christ did on the cross. Of course, there is nothing wrong with doing good things. The truth of the matter is that we are called by Christ to do good works:

> We are God's masterpiece. He has created us anew in Christ Jesus, so we can do the good things he planned for us long ago. (Ephesians 2:10 NLT)

Michael's doing good works was a great thing; it was his understanding of what those works did for him that was incorrect. In other words, the reason why many of us do good works has to change. After all,

> Being a Christian is about who we are as a result of what Jesus Christ did on the cross. >

how can the world look at us and understand who Christ is if both Christian and non-Christians alike have the same misunderstanding about Christianity, the same false idea that faith is all about the things we do and not who we are because of Christ? The world must understand why we are who we are. We are Christians because we are saved and loved by Jesus. So stop to ask yourself the question, *What am I marked by? My works? Or by Jesus?*

Faith-Fueled Courage

DON LOUGH
Word of Life Fellowship, Schroon Lake, NY

Have you ever taken a stand against social injustice? That kind of activism is on the rise, especially among your generation. Many individuals are standing up to defend those people society has attacked or ignored. And while it has become popular to take up certain causes, it still takes great courage to champion God's causes. So let me en*courage* you right now with three examples of how you might take a stand.

COURAGE TO STAND UP

In Scripture, the epitome of courage is David, the shepherd boy who faced Goliath. We're all familiar with this story to one degree or another. We remember that David was little and Goliath was big. We remember that Goliath had a giant ego and a giant sword to match. But we may not remember that David's choice to face Goliath was not very popular. Why? Because David was too young. He was also untrained and therefore ill-prepared. He was not the right guy to be fighting that battle. But he fought anyway . . . because no one else did.

Many of you are fighting battles that my generation has been too afraid to fight ourselves. In your zealous youth, you are attacking the giants that we've let mock our God for years. You are *standing up*. Good for you. Shame on us.

COURAGE TO STAND DOWN

David's fight with Goliath was an impressive display of courage, but another scene from his life shows even more bravery. Saul, the reigning king of Israel, quickly became jealous of David's new popularity. In a blind rage, he tried to spear David. Twice. In just a few short days, David went from being the most popular man in Israel to a fugitive running for his life. It wasn't fair, but Saul was obsessed with hunting David down. He chased David into the

Wilderness of En Gedi as if David were an animal. In 1 Samuel 24:2–4, David had an ideal opportunity to strike back. Saul unknowingly wandered into the same cave where David and his men were hiding. David's men were pumped. They thought it was finally time for David to settle the score. But it was at this moment that David showed the courage to *stand down* in the face of injustice. First Samuel 18:14 pays tribute to David, saying he "behaved wisely in all his ways, and the Lord was with him." He was brave enough to step in and defend others, but even more impressive, he was willing to experience injustice without responding with revenge. Such courage is clear evidence of extreme trust in God. Such courage means that the person believes God will defend him even when it seems unlikely or even impossible.

Courage—the stand-up kind and the stand-down kind—is admirable, but only one of these two types of courage is popular. It's become very trendy to *oppose* injustice, but not to *endure* despite it. Rare is the student who knows how to endure suffering.

> He was brave enough to step in and defend others; he was willing to experience injustice without responding with revenge. **>**

COURAGE TO SPEAK OUT

Eventually someone did lash out against Saul, but it wasn't David. An opportunistic young soldier happened across a wounded Saul one day and seized what he thought would be a career-making moment. Forever, he believed, he would be known as the king slayer, and he expected David, Saul's chief rival, to be pleased. But he was wrong. Second Samuel 1:14 records David's response to King Saul's murderer. He said, "How was it you were not afraid to put forth your hand to destroy the Lord's anointed?"

Sometimes obeying God is a messy business. His way is rarely convenient, and it's not always easy. Consider that David was about to inherit a fractured nation on the brink of civil war. It would have been simpler to pat the king-slayer kid on the back, make a new friend, and move on. But David couldn't do it. He knew the murder was wrong, and David was not a person prone to ignore sin. Not in himself; not in those around him. David felt compelled to speak up, and it didn't matter that the right thing was inconvenient or hard.

Sometimes obeying God is a messy business. >

When it comes to obeying God, popularity or convenience should not matter. May your courage always be fueled by your faith.

Embracing Your Relationship with God

WILL HAGLE
Mobberly Baptist Church, Longview, TX

I t's a three-step process, but maybe one you haven't thought much about. I'm talking about spiritual growth and the cycle of Discovery ☞ Ownership ☞ Leadership. Here are some details.

Discovery is the very first step toward knowing the things of God. Listening to a sermon, attending a small group, reading the Bible—these are avenues of discovery. And I'd say we have this down pretty well. You probably have no problem finding opportunities to discover spiritual things. You can go to various worship services, conferences, concerts, and even church coffeehouses to gain new spiritual insights. After you discover a spiritual principle, the next step is *ownership*. This is the stage I want to discuss here.

First, let me tell you why I believe ownership of your faith is critical. In the past few years, statistics have shown that a great number of Christian teens abandon the church and their walk with God when they go off to college, and I think the lack of spiritual ownership is a reason for this trend. Students who fail to take responsibility for their personal spiritual growth become distant from God when they go off to college and Mom and Dad aren't there to wake them up for church. Then, in addition to missing church, these students neglect their quiet time because no one is encouraging them to spend time alone with God. It doesn't take long to drift from God, and that happens to any of us who fail to own our relationship with Christ. After all, how can you have a thriving relationship with Someone you don't spend time with? That said, I can assure you that I have seen hundreds of students who *have* owned their faith, who leave home and stay close to Christ throughout college and into life.

But back to the topic. The moment you decide to become a follower of Jesus

How can you have a thriving relationship with Someone you don't spend time with? >

Christ is the moment you begin a personal relationship with Him. This decision to follow Christ is a personal decision: only you can make this decision; no one else can do it for you. And when you make that decision, the Bible clearly teaches, you must mean it with your heart (Romans 10:9). In fact, I think the same can be said of every other spiritual thing we do: we must have the right purpose in our hearts. This is *spiritual ownership.*

Let me explain. Think of spiritual ownership as embracing every aspect of your relationship with God and every truth about Him that you discover. The word *ownership* means "taking as one's own; to possess." It's critical that you take your relationship with Christ as your own and wholeheartedly possess it. It's critical that you take the biblical principles you discover as your own and possess them. Your parents can pray for you, but they cannot pray in your place. Your grandma can have a thriving relationship with Christ, but she can't have your relationship with Christ for you. Your youth minister can have a thousand amazing stories about God, but his stories will not sustain you. Take ownership of your relationship with Christ and live that out. And when you do, you'll soon have your own faith stories!

When I was a small child, my grandmother would give me a dollar or some pocket change to put in the offering plate at church. Was I giving that money to God with the right purpose in my heart? No. In fact, it wasn't even my money. But my grandmother was helping me learn a biblical principle. I eventually *discovered* that tithing is giving to God. Later on in my life I took full-on *ownership* of this principle and began to purposefully give back to God: He has given me everything, and I want to follow His plan and give 10 percent to the church. But what happens when a person tithes who is not taking ownership? You don't have to look far in the Bible to find this. Go read the story of Cain and Abel (Genesis 4).

So how can I know when students are taking ownership of their relationship with Christ? I see them reading their Bibles, praying, and memorizing Scripture on their own, without anyone telling them to. These actions suggest that they have seen for themselves the value of their relationship with Jesus, and they are choosing to spend time with Him. Think about it. When you bow your head to pray, are you praying out of reverence and honor for God? Are you speaking to Him from your heart, or are you acting out of habit? When you sing a worship song, are you praising God from your heart, or are you just going through the motions, not really even thinking about what the words mean and certainly not singing the words to God?

Ownership is embracing as truly your own every aspect of your relationship with God and every truth about Him that you discover. Ownership means you take responsibility for your personal spiritual growth. Ownership means you stand on the truth of every biblical principle you discover. Then you will be ready to use your influence and lead based on your confidence of who He is and who you are in Him—and you can read about that kind of spiritual leadership on page 205.

SCRIPTURES THAT ENCOURAGE OWNERSHIP

* Matthew 22:36–40
* Luke 9:23
* 2 Peter 1:5–7

A Serious Case of Apathy

JORDAN EASLEY
Long Hollow Baptist Church, Hendersonville, TN

World War II second lieutenant had graduated from Harvard before entering the military. His first assignment was to convince a group of raw recruits from the hills of Oklahoma that they should purchase GI life insurance: the US government would pay their families ten thousand dollars if they died while on duty. With his uniform pressed and his speech eloquent, he appealed to these men and their responsibilities, to the love of their families and their loyalty to their country.

He ended his presentation by asking, "So, how many of you will buy the GI life insurance before you go overseas?" Nobody responded, so he repeated himself in a much louder voice. After again getting no response and beginning to lose his composure, the lieutenant saw the master sergeant suddenly walk into the room. Seeing what was going on, he put his hand on the lieutenant's shoulder and said, "Let me talk with the boys. I don't think you've convinced them they have a need."

"Gentlemen," he said, "it's like this: You don't buy the insurance, you go overseas, you get a bullet in the head, and the government doesn't have to come up with anything. Or you buy the insurance, you go overseas, you get a bullet in the head, and the government has to come up with ten thousand big ones. Now tell me, gentlemen, whom do you think the government will send to the front lines first?"

They sold some insurance!

Like those GIs and the insurance policy, people all around us are rejecting Jesus because they don't think they need Him. They think they can get along just fine without Him. Yet, if you've been in church awhile, you know we're supposed to tell people about Jesus. But for some reason, this command of God has lost its urgency. We've become apathetic to the things of God even as we journey through life with Him.

God loves us. And we love God. And everyone is searching for love. The Bible talks a lot about love: Scripture is clear that we are to love one another.

> **We've become apathetic to the things of God even as we journey through life with Him.** >

First John 4:10–12 says, "This is love: not that we loved God, but that he loved us and sent his Son as an atoning sacrifice for our sins. Dear friends, since God so loved us, we also ought to love one another. No one has ever seen God; but if we love one another, God lives in us and his love is made complete in us" (NIV).

Jesus said that the greatest commandment is to "'love the LORD your God with all your heart, with all your soul, and with all your mind.' . . . And the second [greatest commandment] is like it: 'You shall to love your neighbor as yourself'" (Matthew 22:37, 39). Jesus also said, "A new commandment I give to you, that you love one another; as I have loved you, that you also love one another" (John 13:34).

The Great Commandment is a call to love, but for whatever reason, many of us Christians don't. We don't have a genuine love in our hearts for the lost or the needy or the dirty or the hungry. When we find ourselves guilty of a lack of love and apathetic to the very things God instructs us to take seriously, we need to reevaluate God's commands and our response.

Read the risen Christ's words in Revelation 3:14–19 (NCV):

The Amen, the faithful and true witness, the ruler of all God has made, says this: "I know what you do, that you are not hot or cold. I wish that you were hot or cold! But because you are lukewarm—neither hot, nor cold—I am ready to spit you out of my mouth. You say, 'I am rich, and I have become wealthy and do not need anything.' But you do not know that you are really miserable, pitiful, poor, blind, and naked. I advise you to buy from me gold made pure in fire so you can be truly rich. Buy from me white clothes so you can be clothed and so you can cover your shameful nakedness. Buy from me medicine to put on your eyes so you can truly see.

"I correct and punish those whom I love. So be eager to do right, and change your hearts and lives."

When we're apathetic, we're pathetic because we don't care. Jesus wants us to care, and He wants us to love. He wants us to love Him, and He wants us to love others. It's easy to live with blinders on, oblivious to our surroundings. We're naturally self-centered people, but when our self-centeredness takes over our lives, we not only become unaware of those around us, but we also lose sight of our true purpose on this earth. Our hearts are beating today because God lets them beat. He allowed us to wake up this morning because He's not yet through using us on the earth for His purposes and His glory.

So we're surrounded by people who may not even know they have a need, and it's our job to love them enough to share the good news with them. God doesn't have a plan B. He commands us to love, and being apathetic toward God truly is the antithesis to loving Him. We can't do what we were designed to do if we don't care enough about God or people to obey God. That's why God says to either be hot or cold, not lukewarm. He wants us to make a choice—to either love Him or not, to either obey Him or not. Will we be hot or cold?

It's not time for us believers to check out. It's time for us to wake up! We are to love like God loves and look for opportunities to serve Him by serving others— and we're to do so today.

(Spiritual) Identity Theft

MICHAEL HEAD
Second Baptist Houston, Houston, TX

We've all heard about identity theft—and we all hope it doesn't happen to us. Yet I have grown comfortable paying the majority of our bills online. I find it convenient, and I trust the safeguards currently in place. Still, incidents of various types of identity theft have more than doubled over the past years and now represent the leading consumer fraud reported to the Federal Trade Commission.

Many identity fraud cases begin with the simple theft of a credit card number, and that can be done by simply copying the information from a paper receipt. Stolen credit cards and Social Security numbers (SSN) can devastate a person's life. When thieves effectively steal your identity, they can do one or all of the following:

* Open new credit card accounts using your name, birth date, and SSN.
* Call your credit card company pretending to be you and change the mailing address.
* Establish cellular phone service in your name.
* Open a bank account in your name and write bad checks on that account.

The real tragedy of identity theft is that you may not realize that it has happened to you until billing cycles pass and you don't receive a statement or you do receive bills for a credit card you never had, a bad credit report that lists debts you never incurred, or charges on your credit card bills that you did not authorize. Identity theft can be very subtle in the beginning, and before you know it, you find yourself having to prove your identity.

Something more important than theft of our money and credit identity, however, happens every second on a spiritual level. As a matter of fact, it has been happening since the beginning of time. Satan is the guilty party, the original identity thief who loves to take the image of God in you and mess it up, drain your spirit, and, by doing so, make you look nothing at all like Christ. Spiritual identity theft occurs when the enemy robs you of who you are in Christ. Jesus clearly taught that truth—"The thief does not come except to steal, and to kill, and to destroy: I have come that they might have life, and that they might have it more abundantly" (John 10:10). We know who our enemy is.

One of the ways this enemy Satan steals your identity is by reminding you of your past. When he tries that approach, stand in this truth: "If anyone is in Christ, he is a new creation; old things have passed away; behold, all things have become new" (2 Corinthians 5:17). When you accepted Christ, you became a new creation. The old you is gone! You still have the same body, but the old inner you has been replaced by the new. So when Satan tries to remind you of your past, you can respond by reminding him of his future! (God wins; Satan loses—and he loses big-time.)

> Spiritual identity theft occurs when the enemy robs you of who you are in Christ. >

So what can you do to protect yourself from spiritual identity theft?

1. BELIEVE THE WORD OF THE LIVING GOD!

And in God's Word Paul declared this important reality about himself and about every other person who names Jesus as Savior and Lord: "I have been crucified with Christ; it is no longer I who live, but Christ lives in me; and the life which I now live in the flesh I live by faith in the Son of God, who loved me and gave Himself for me" (Galatians 2:20). You are a new creation in Jesus.

2. NEVER ACCEPT THE LIMITATIONS OTHERS WANT TO PUT ON YOUR LIFE!

Sometimes the most well-meaning people will try to keep you from doing what you know God has for you to do! Don't listen to them. Stay focused on Jesus and follow Him! That may be easier to do if you remember this truth:

> **Stay focused on Jesus and follow Him! >**

> There is therefore now no condemnation to those who are in Christ Jesus. . . . For the law of the Spirit of life in Christ Jesus has made me free from the law of sin and death. For what the law could not do in that it was weak through the flesh, God did by sending His own Son in the likeness of sinful flesh, on account of sin: He condemned sin in the flesh, that the righteous requirement of the law might be fulfilled in us who do not walk according to the flesh but according to the Spirit. (Romans 8:1–4)

3. STOP UNCOVERING WHAT JESUS HAS ALREADY BURIED!

And Jesus has buried the old you:

> If Christ is in you, your body is dead because of sin, yet your spirit is alive because of righteousness. And if the Spirit of him who raised Jesus from the dead is living in you, he who raised Christ from the dead will also give life to your mortal bodies through his Spirit, who lives in you. Therefore, brothers, we have an obligation—but it is not to the sinful nature, to live according to it. (Romans 8:10–12 NIV)

Are you the victim of spiritual identity theft? If so, then go to Jesus now for a brand-new ID in Him!

Starting Over—By God's Grace

> MATT PETTY
> Burnt Hickory Baptist Church, Powder Springs, GA

D o you ever feel like it would be nice to be able to start over? What if we could have a redo? Or, better yet, what if we could use what we know now, jump into a time machine, and then start over? Part of me wishes that I lived in the movies so this could happen, because in the real world it's impossible. We cannot undo or change the past, nor can we make excuses for the past that carry any weight. We may not be able to redo our past, but those of us who have given our life to Jesus have the ability to start over.

> In its purest form, salvation is God giving us a new beginning. >

In its purest form, salvation is God giving us a new beginning. His continual forgiveness gives us an eternal freshness. God set up a system of sacrifices that offered people both a way to have their sins covered and a symbolic new start for the year. If you look at the journey of God's chosen people—the nation of Israel—through the Old Testament, you will see that they were masters at the art of starting over. They would allow God to rule for a while . . . but then, in the same chapter, turn back to their wicked ways . . . and then two years later turn back to God. And remember Jonah? He started over the hard way after he was spit out of the mouth of a great fish. Rarely will you find a section of Scripture that does not directly or indirectly point toward the opportunity God gives people to allow Him to have their life and give them a new start.

But I don't think the question most of us are asking is, "Does God give us the ability to start over?" The real question is, "How?" How do we get a new start? How do we stop walking the path we're on and go another direction? One person in Scripture who clearly answers that question for us is the apostle Paul. He put it like this: "One thing I do: Forgetting what is behind and straining toward what is ahead, I press on toward the goal to win the prize for which God has called me heavenward in Christ Jesus" (Philippians 3:13–14 NIV).

Any other system of forgiveness or new starts in Scripture is only temporary. The sacrifices of the Old Testament, the blessings of prophets, and even messages from angels are all passing. The only newness that will last rests on the cross and the resurrection of Jesus Christ. So how do we walk in that newness every day? Paul summed up the process: "forget what's behind and strain toward what's ahead." From his jail cell he looked at all the things that had happened in his life and said, "Forget about what you've done or haven't done and move forward." Why did he say this? Because Satan will bring to our minds past success to make us lazy or prideful, unwilling to approach God, or he will remind us of our past failures to make us ashamed, afraid, and reluctant to approach God. Listening to and acting on the thoughts Satan puts in our minds will result in idle and godless living. Will you resolve to start over, to "strain toward what is ahead," no matter the cost? Since that is God's calling, you can be absolutely sure the effort will be worth it—and to Him be the praise!

Once you and I are able to let go of the past, we can then move toward the future. Let's look at three action items that can guide our pressing on to the goal:

* **Get perspective!** Look at what Paul said earlier: "I consider everything a loss compared to . . . knowing Christ Jesus" (Philippians 3:8 NIV). *Everything* means there is no exception. Yet if anyone could have put felt confident about his godly Jewish life, it would be Paul. He was from the right family, he was well educated, he grew up in the right place, he obeyed all the laws, he hung out with the right group of people, and he

persecuted the Christians better than anyone (see Philippians 3:4–6). But Paul got off the throne of his life and allowed God to have it. We need to do the same.

* **Experience power**. Paul not only wanted to know Christ; Paul wanted to know Christ's power, the very same power that raised Him from the dead (see Philippians 3:10–11). The word *know* means more than having information stored in our mind. *Know* literally means that we want to experience God's power, and this has to be firsthand. We cannot strain toward what's ahead if we're somehow depending on other people's experience of God's love and power. Each of us has to make a personal decision to receive the salvation and accompanying power that God offers. No one can receive our salvation for us. God definitely desires all of us to walk in His full power, but He is not the limiting factor. He is not keeping us from living in His power. We are.

* **Live as who we are**, and we are sons and daughters of the King. It's not enough to claim to be a follower of Christ. If we have truly given our hearts to Jesus, we must learn to live out what He has called us to be. Mark Batterson says it like this in his book *Primal*: "Christianity was never intended to be a noun. And when we turn it into a noun it becomes a turnoff. Christianity was always intended to be a verb. We have got to act on God ideas and obey the promptings of the Holy Spirit. Talk is cheap."[1]

You wanna start over? Forget what's behind and press on toward what's ahead. God will do the rest.

#decisions &

discipleship

Do You Have a Compass?

> RIC GARLAND
> Word of Life Fellowship, Schroon Lake, NY

Lying could be more Christian than telling the truth. Stealing could be better than respecting private property. No action is good or right in itself. It depends on whether it hurts or helps people, whether or not it serves love's purpose—understanding love to be a personal concern—in the situation.

—JOSEPH FLETCHER, CREATOR OF SITUATION ETHICS

Okay, so how did you react to that statement? Did you have to read it twice? Did the phrase *situation ethics* make you bristle? Whatever your reaction, the truth is that this way of thinking has subtly—or maybe not so subtly—entered the Christian community. "Thou shalt not commit adultery"—ordinarily. "Thou shalt not steal"—usually. And "Honor [by obeying] your mother and father"—generally.

Simply put, situational ethics says that right and wrong depend on the situation. Nothing is always wrong, and nothing is always right. That call depends on the situation. To say it another way, "If it feels good, do it as long as you don't hurt anybody."

Biblical integrity, however, is a fixed devotion to the Bible's principles of right and wrong. Biblical integrity maintains that moral absolutes exist. That means that some things are always wrong and some things are always right. And biblical integrity asserts that, for every situation, God's Word has a principle we should live by. We don't make decisions according to the situation but according to our sovereign God.

Situational ethics and biblical integrity cannot both be right. The two are mutually exclusive. Below are some guidelines to help you choose biblical integrity.

168

STEP 1: CHANGE YOUR BELIEFS

What's right? What's wrong?

* **Experience:** some people base their beliefs about right and wrong on what they have experienced, and that makes truth relative, not absolute.
* **Example:** others base their beliefs on what they see in people around them like their parents or coach.
* **Emotions:** some people say, "If it feels good, do it." Right and wrong is all about how you feel.
* **God's Word:** as Christians we must build our beliefs about right and wrong on the Word of God.

John 17:17 tells us that we are made holy by truth and that God's Word is truth, not our experiences, the examples around us, or our emotions. So change your beliefs about right and wrong so that they are based only upon the Word of God.

STEP 2: CHANGE YOUR POWER SOURCE

Who are you plugged into for strength? Most of us like to be self-sufficient. "I can do it on my own" is our motto. But the Bible says that you can do all things *through* Christ who gives you strength (Philippians 4:13).

So who or what are you plugged into for your strength to live the Christian life? If you choose biblical integrity, here's what can result:

1. It can give you courage (Psalm 41:11–12).
2. It can give you a sense of security (Proverbs 10:9).
3. It can keep you from being overwhelmed by sin (Proverbs 13:6).
4. God will be pleased with how you live your life (1 Chronicles 29:17).
5. God will give you more influence and greater responsibility (Nehemiah 7:2).
6. It will give you direction (Proverbs 11:3).

STEP 3: CHANGE YOUR STRATEGY

If you don't live with God's Word as your foundation, the following will result:

1. **Double-Mindedness:** You will be a person with a divided allegiance, so it won't be easy to make the right choices.
2. **Desire:** You'll often make choices according to your feelings.
3. **Deception:** When you make decisions according to feelings, you won't easily see the consequences of your sin.
4. **Disobedience:** When it feels right and you either don't see any consequences of your choice or you rationalize away those consequences, it's easy to sin.
5. **Death:** Sin starts out feeling so good, but it always ends in death! When you sin, you kill your character and your reputation.

So what's the right strategy for making choices about right and wrong?

1. JUST DECIDE IT!

Stop being double-minded. That's where it all starts. Make a decision to give your all to God and to live the way He wants you to live.

James 1:5 says that God is willing to give you wisdom and the ability to make the right choices. So if you decide to give Him everything, all you have to do is ask!

2. JUST DIG IN TO IT!

Wisdom comes from God, and He gives wisdom in His Word. Be faithful about having a daily time for reading God's Word and praying (James 1:23–25).

3. JUST DO IT!

Discipline yourself to live by the wisdom God gives (James 1:21–22).

Biblical integrity means that you allow the Spirit of God to use the Word of God as a compass to direct and change your life.

Following Christ in a Fan-Based World

KEN BURNETT
Fellowship of Christian Athletes, Huntsville, AL

I am a fan of many foods, most music, and all sports. It does, however, concern me how crazy we fans have become. This became a reality to me when I attended a football game in a huge dome. The announcer asked all of us to stand and remain standing for a moment of silence for the family and friends of a twenty-year-old young man who, the night before, had fallen from the third level of the building to his death. He actually landed on someone, but that person survived with minor injuries.

I prayed for this young man's family while I stood, but I was also frustrated that something like this could even happen. I hurt for this dear family and this group of friends who lost someone they loved. Yet it blew me away to look around this enormous building and think that at one moment a fan was cheering for his favorite team and the next moment he was falling into eternity. Witnesses reported to news media that he was drinking alcohol for hours before the game even though he wasn't old enough to buy it. If this is true, I wonder how the person who made the purchase must feel. Fans are out of control! (At times I'm just embarrassed to be human.)

Now, our dear country and the world at large offer many idols that we can be fans of. Being a *fan* is not always a bad thing unless we put whatever we're celebrating and its pursuit of it before our relationship with God. (For years I've told people that a guy or a girl can be great, but that person will always be a terrible god.)

Do you struggle to be a follower of Christ in our fan-based world? Probably so. At least from time to time. Look at two facts we often see in *fans*:

1. *Fans* are often all about *feelings.*
2. *Fans* are often very *foolish.*

Have you ever noticed the change in fans when, midgame, their winning team starts to lose? Fans can start to be real mean-spirited toward their team. Fans who allow themselves to go up and down as the game unfolds are following their feelings. Once I watched an ESPN special that showed fights before, during, and after NFL games. It has actually gotten so bad that the organization FAV has been created. FAV stands for Fans Against Violence. Can you see how foolish we fans have become? We can't control our feelings about a game, so fights break out and some of us end up in jail. Fans today are often all about their feelings . . . and that often leads them to make foolish decisions.

So how do we follow Christ in this fan-based world? I'm glad you asked! Look at this story from Luke 17:11–19 for a hint:

> Now it happened as He went to Jerusalem that He passed through the midst of Samaria and Galilee. Then as He entered a certain village, there met Him ten men who were lepers, who stood afar off. And they lifted up their voices and said, "Jesus, Master, have mercy on us!"
>
> So when He saw them, He said to them, "Go, show yourselves to the priests." And so it was that as they went, they were cleansed.
>
> And one of them, when he saw that he was healed, returned, and with a loud voice glorified God, and fell down on his face at His feet, giving Him thanks. And he was a Samaritan.
>
> So Jesus answered and said, "Were there not ten cleansed? But where are the nine? Were there not any found who returned to give glory to God except this foreigner?" And He said to him, "Arise, go your way. Your faith has made you well."

What did it take for this fan to become a player on Jesus' team? I call it an "attitude of gratitude." When you and I experience God's healing of our past, how can we do anything but seek Him out daily and praise Him loudly? When God saves us from our sins, we not only become a part of His family, but we also realize we have been picked to be on His team.

And there is definitely a difference between players and fans. Players have pride in who they play for. Notice that the only one who returned to give God praise did not care what others thought. He took pride in doing what was right.

Players not only take pride in being on the team, but players also prepare for the battle ahead of time. Friend, no matter how old you live to be, you and I never can fight the good fight for Jesus without preparing for the battle. We do this by being in God's Word daily.

Players have *pride*, players *prepare*, and players have *passion*! Notice in the passage how the healed leper praised God with a loud voice and threw himself at Jesus' feet. I am not suggesting we have to fall down before God during our

> Players have *pride*, players *prepare*, and players have *passion*! **>**

worship, nor should we try to bring ourselves attention by being the loudest one during worship. As God's children, though, we should be unashamed to let others know who we follow. "Though nine do not go with me . . . I still will follow!" That's PASSION!

Do you desire to follow Christ in this fan-based world? Then start today by asking His forgiveness for being a fan of this world and thank Jesus for choosing you to be part of His family. You and I are to play on Christ's team, not just watch from the bleachers! May we live and play for Him so all will see we have an attitude of gratitude!

God's Guidelines for the Gray Areas of Life

DR. DANNY AKIN
Southeastern Theological Seminary, Wake Forest, NC

Ethical decision making in the twenty-first century is challenging— and that's an understatement. A Christ-centered biblical perspective is demanded, and a genuinely Christian mind-set is required if we are to live as God's people in God's world.

Embracing biblical principles that are true anywhere, anytime, and under any circumstances will help us live out the gospel of Jesus Christ. A great place to discover these strategies is the New Testament book of 1 Corinthians. Here was a church gone wild! Believers were struggling to be faithful Christ-followers in a radically secular, immoral, non-Christian context. Paul wrote to them in order to teach them how to live for Jesus. He set forth a number of universal, nonnegotiable principles that enable us to engage our culture with integrity while staying true to the gospel of Jesus Christ. The following ten principles speak to those who lived in the first century as well as those of us who live in the twenty-first century.

1. WILL THIS ACTION BE HELPFUL TO ME? (1 Corinthians 6:12; 10:23) Certain actions are simply not helpful for believers. So ask yourself, *Is a particular activity helpful, or profitable, or beneficial? Will it strengthen my relationship with Christ and build me up?*

2. WILL THIS ACTION POTENTIALLY ENSLAVE ME?
(1 Corinthians 6:12)
We are to be a slave to only one Master. His name is Jesus. So choose to live a radically Christ-centered life because you belong to Him.

Also, realize that true spiritual freedom is not the right to do what you want. Spiritual freedom is experiencing the supernatural enablement of Christ to do what you ought to do and to enjoy doing so! We must guard against any action that will potentially enslave us.

3. WILL THIS ACTION ENCOURAGE OTHERS? (1 Corinthians 8:13; 10:24, 32)

We should be willing, for the sake of others, to adjust our lives that we might not hurt or harm. This principle reflects the mind of Christ (Philippians 2:3–5). For the sake of your community of faith, "consider others as more important than yourselves" (v. 3 HCSB). The gospel demands that the needs of others outweigh our own.

4. WILL THIS ACTION HELP OR HINDER MY GOSPEL WITNESS? (1 Corinthians 9:12, 19–23; 10:32–33)

This principle is so crucial that Paul repeated it three different times. The bottom line is this: nothing in our words or deeds must hinder or obscure the gospel!

5. IS THIS ACTION CONSISTENT WITH MY NEW LIFE IN CHRIST? (1 Corinthians 6:9–11, 19)

Sometimes in our desire to communicate the gospel clearly and without unnecessary information, we go too far and actually miscommunicate the message. We can adjust our vocabulary, compromise purity, and inadvertently hide the glorious gospel that transforms and changes lives. Our new life demands that we proclaim and live the message with holiness, boldness, accuracy, and humility.

6. WILL THIS ACTION VIOLATE MY CONSCIENCE?

(1 Corinthians 10:28–29)

It is dangerous to ignore the inner voice of conscience. It is God-given, and it is under redemptive reconstruction through the Spirit and the Word. A well-informed, Scripture-saturated, Spirit-sensitive conscience will warn us of things that are sinful, evil, and unwise.

But Paul would not say, "Let your conscience be your guide," as if conscience by itself is a sufficient umpire when it comes to good decision making. Rather, Paul would say, "Let your conscience *guided by Scripture* and *controlled by God's love* be your guide."

7. WILL THIS ACTION FOLLOW THE PATTERN OF JESUS' LIFE? (1 Corinthians 11:1)

To live like Jesus you must know Jesus! Researcher George Barna says most Christians don't *act* like Jesus because they don't *think* like Jesus. Getting to know Jesus better enables us to think more like Him, and then we will be better prepared to pursue a "pattern of life" that looks like the life Jesus led.

8. WILL THIS ACTION SHOW LOVE TO OTHERS?

(1 Corinthians 13:1–7)

Love is the magnet that attracts others to Christ. It is the fulcrum that balances freedom and responsibility, belief and behavior. If our actions are not grounded in love, it does not matter what we know about Jesus, say about Him, or do for Him.

9. WILL THIS ACTION HONOR MY BODY, WHICH BELONGS TO GOD? (1 Corinthians 6:19–20)

We are not our own; we have been bought with a price by God through Jesus' blood on Calvary. John Piper says six things are true because Jesus bought your body: (1) God is for the body, not against it. (2) The body is the dwelling place of the Holy Spirit. (3) The body will be resurrected from the dead. (4) The body is not to be mastered by anything but Christ. (5) The body is not to be used for any immorality. (6) The body is to be used for the glory of God. Piper said this: "Use your body in ways that will show that God is more satisfying, more precious, more to be desired, more glorious than anything the body craves."[1]

10. WILL THIS ACTION GLORIFY GOD? (1 Corinthians 10:31)

This climactic and overarching principle has been called "the joyful duty of man." It is right in its God-focus, for He is the most beautiful and valuable Being in the entire universe. This principle is also right in its human perspective, for it makes clear why we are here: to live for God's glory. No part of life is exempt from this principle. It is comprehensive, and following it is satisfying!

Dig Wells or Build Fences?

BRENT CROWE
Student Leadership University, Orlando, FL

Sometime ago in the Australian outback, ranchers faced an unusual dilemma. Due to the vast acreage many of them owned, they found their time consumed by mending and repairing fences. The fences were designed, of course, to keep the cows on their own land. Yet because of the miles and miles of fences, the ranchers spent the vast majority of their time focusing on the boundaries of their properties rather than the welfare of the cattle.

These ranchers soon realized that focusing on the fences was actually self-defeating: they spent so much time on the outskirts of their properties that they were neglecting the livestock, and the result was unproductive ranches. The solution? The ranchers began to dig wells at strategic locations on their land. Their assumption was that the livestock would never stray too far from these precious water sources. The plan worked, and the ranchers were able to focus more time and energy on the livestock, and this time the result was more productive ranches.[1]

The questions below are intended to help you focus on wells of wisdom rather than boundaries of right and wrong. We must be careful not to fixate on the boundary between what is permissible and what is sinful. Freedom in Christ, when properly understood, is actually a much higher standard. In Paul's words, "All things are lawful for me, but not all things are helpful; all things are lawful for me, but not all things edify" (1 Corinthians 10:23).

Each of us will face thousands of decisions that we won't have a chapter and verse for. Scripture, for instance, doesn't speak directly and specifically to many of our entertainment choices, our relationship choices, or social media etiquette. So what are we to do? We are to "test all things" (1 Thessalonians

  • • • • • • • • • • • • • • • • • •

5:21), and we are to rely on God's Word as a "lamp to [our] feet" (Psalm 119:105). But how exactly how are we to test everything? And how is the Bible a lamp unto our feet when we are not given a chapter or a verse for every one of life's decisions?

First, remember that the Bible is not limited to just yes and no answers concerning good and evil. Rather, God's Word shapes our thinking and prepares us for

> God's Word shapes our thinking and prepares us for any and all decisions we'll face. >

any and all decisions we'll face. In other words, the Bible doesn't just teach us *what* to think and believe; it also informs *how we are to think and believe.* The sixteen questions below were published in my book *Chasing Elephants: Wrestling with the Gray Areas of Life.* I hope these questions—that you can apply to any decision the Bible does not specifically address—help you see and appreciate the incredible relevancy of Scripture.

1. Is the decision within the explicit moral will of God?

2. Is the decision being made in the attitude of Christ (Romans 15:1–13)?

3. Is the decision being made under the control of the flesh or the Holy Spirit (Galatians 5:13–26)?

4. Will the decision have a positive spiritual impact on me (1 Corinthians 6:12; 10:23–24)?

5. Will this decision addict or enslave me (1 Corinthians 6:12)?

6. Is the decision consistent with living like Christ?

7. Will the decision hurt a brother or sister spiritually or set a spiritual deathtrap (Romans 14:13)?

8. Will the decision have a positive spiritual impact on fellow believers (Romans 14:19; 1 Corinthians 10:23–24; Galatians 6:1–10)?

9. Does the decision go against my conscience (Romans 14:14)?

10. Will the decision disrupt fellowship and damage relationships within the community (Romans 14:15)?

11. Will the decision damage anyone's reputation (Romans 14:16)?

12. Will the decision move my focus away from the big picture of God's kingdom (Romans 14:17–19)?

13. Is the decision being made out of a selfish heart (Romans 14:20–21)? Will the decision offend anyone (1 Corinthians 10:32)?

14. Can the decision be imitated by others who understand their freedom in Christ (1 Corinthians 10:33–11:1)?

15. Is the decision being made for the cause of evangelism (1 Corinthians 9:19–24; 10:33)?

16. Will the decision glorify God (1 Corinthians 10:31)? Will the decision make a big deal about Jesus (Galatians 6:11–16)?[2]

What's the Point?

CHRIS WHITE
Mobilizing Students, Fayetteville, GA

A few years ago I saw a video clip of a Michael Jackson concert. Hundreds of thousands of screaming fans had gathered to hear the pop phenom sing his hit music. A few moments into the video, Michael himself appeared onstage, and the crowd lost it! They went nuts! Girls were screaming, crying, shaking, yelling, passing out—completely overwhelmed by the presence of their favorite pop icon. The crowd seemed to move in unison as it swayed back and forth to their favorite songs. Some fans were crushed by the weight of the crowd pushing them toward the stage, all hungry to get a glimpse, a touch, a drop of sweat, or just a closer view of the one they adored . . . Michael. This went on for about five minutes, and I thought to myself, *True worship . . . false god!*

You know what struck me most about this video? The picture of true, authentic, heartfelt worship I saw. But as uninhibited and wholehearted as it was, the worship wasn't directed toward the right object, which made it false worship or—as the Bible would say—idolatry. We human beings were created by God to worship *Him*. He wired us to give 100 percent of ourselves to living in overwhelming, awe-inspiring, all-consuming delight and fellowship with the One who made us. Nothing can satisfy our deepest cravings for intimacy, friendship, and love the way He can. So when we direct all our affection, time, money, and energy toward something other

> When we direct all our affection, time, money, and energy toward something other than God, that thing becomes an idol. >

than God, that thing becomes an idol. It falls far short of God's holy and divine glory.

When I was growing up, I thought worship was the thirty minutes of music before the pastor stepped up to preach. Wow! What an incredibly small view of worship that was! I later realized that to reduce worship to just music—or to a traditional or contemporary style, or to my favorite songs sung by my favorite worship band, or to thirty minutes a week on Sunday—is a far cry from what the Bible teaches.

You see, worship is so much more than music. Worship is all encompassing. It's not what I do during a Sunday morning service or one evening a week. Worship is what I do with my life, with every moment of every day every day of the week. Worship is life! Everything we do flows out of what we worship, making everything we do an act of worship. Everything.

> **Everything we do flows out of what we worship, making everything we do an act of worship. Everything. >**

Think about it. Why do we praise guys like LeBron James or Drew Brees? It's because of their intense pursuit of something they're passionate about. They have given themselves sacrificially to a game with such single-minded focus that their performance leaves everyone awed and inspired. And God made worship that easy: just give yourself wholeheartedly to something or someone. But your effort falls short if your object of worship is not what you were created to worship. You will experience only an incredible emptiness if you worship anyone or anything other than Christ. That's why Michael Jordan came back to the NBA three separate times after retiring: all the fame and money in the world apparently didn't satisfy him. And one day your favorite pop icon will die, or you'll get an injury or become too old to play your favorite sport, or all the smarts in the world will not impress you anymore. The list of things people worship only to be disappointed is endless, because things and people were not created to satisfy us. God made them for our enjoyment, but not to be worshipped. I am to enjoy my sport, my school, my friends, my family, my kids, my girlfriend/boyfriend, my job . . . but *not* worship them!

In Matthew 22:36–40, we read about a religious leader who asked Jesus which commandments, in all of Jewish law, are the greatest. Jesus' reply is amazing. He said, " 'You shall love the LORD your God with all your heart, with all your soul, and with all your mind' . . . [and] 'You shall love your neighbor as yourself.' " Jesus basically said, "Give yourself—all of yourself, every ounce of your passion and your focus—to God. He's the only worthy object of your life. He is the only One worthy of your worship."

So, what about you? Think about what consumes most of your thoughts, your time, and your money. What have you given yourself 100 percent to? Whatever it is, that's your object of worship, and that's your god. Remember, anything or anyone other than Christ is an idol. We must repent and allow Christ to become our Source of delight and our only Object of worship.

Dear Jesus, I confess I have given myself to _____ for too long. I repent for making something other than You my focus of worship. Please help me devote my entire life to pursuing You above all other things. Be my strength and my deepest delight forevermore. In Jesus' name, Amen.

#leadership

& missions

Making Disciples

JOHN PAUL BASHAM
Liberty Baptist, Hampton, VA

I t's April 6, 1862, and after a successful first attack on the Union forces of Major General Ulysses S. Grant, you've learned that your leader, General Albert Sidney Johnston, has been killed by a stray bullet. With Union reinforcements on the way and your opposition forces backed into a corner, the outcome of tomorrow's battle seams bleak.

Unfortunately, many Christians feel similar hopelessness as they face the challenges and struggles of everyday life—without solid, biblical guidance. And leadership in the war against Satan and his counterparts is even more crucial then leadership on the battlefield. That's one reason why Jesus calls every believer to Christian leadership:

> Go therefore and make disciples of all nations, baptizing them in the name of the Father and of the Son and of the Holy Spirit, teaching them to observe all things that I have commanded you; and lo, I am with you always, even to the end of the age. (Matthew 28:19–20)

Christ's command to His disciples—called the Great Commission—was clear: by the power of the Holy Spirit, they were to take the truth of Christ to the ends of the earth. Fulfilling this call, however, did not mean merely having a simple conversation about the gospel or extending a passing invitation to the nearest church. These men were charged with the task of bringing up the next generation of leaders for the sake of the gospel. Christ had trained them: He had given this first group of leaders the tools and knowledge they needed to advance the kingdom of God in their generation. Now it was their turn to teach the next generation of leaders to learn, obey, and pass on to others all that Jesus had taught them.

As we consider the next generation of believers, we can't help but notice a disconnect between the command Jesus issued two thousand years ago and the response of today's Christians. And maybe that typical response is yours as well. Do you think the responsibility of raising up the next generation of believers lies with "professional" Christians—pastors, evangelists, and missionaries? Do you believe that your obligation is little more than going to church, attending youth group, and sometimes helping people in need? Or maybe you don't think you have the gifts you need to train up leaders for the gospel. And maybe the enemy has convinced you that you are not worthy—or old enough—to teach anyone the truths of Scripture.

Despite our feelings of inadequacy, each one of us is commanded to not only share the truth of Jesus Christ with others but also help fellow believers learn to do the same. As Charles Spurgeon said, "A whetstone, though it cannot cut, may sharpen a knife that will." God has often chosen men and women without power and prestige to accomplish His will, and sometimes God brings greatness from simplicity. When God spoke to Moses and asked him to lead His people out of Egypt, Moses expressed his feelings of inadequacy (Exodus 3). But God wouldn't take no for an answer, and Moses must have worried about his weaknesses. Yet God provided all that Moses needed and saw him through his assignment every step of the way. God will do the same for those who obey Jesus' Great Commission today.

What are you doing to be sure you are trained and able to do what Jesus commands—to both share the gospel and enable others to share the gospel? You and your generation are crucial to the future of the church, and you are among the gatekeepers to the hearts of your peers. So, again, what are you doing to protect and grow in your relationship with Jesus? And what are you doing to learn how to lead others into a dynamic and intimate walk with Him?

God has called all who thirst to go to Him and be satisfied: "Incline your ear, and come to Me. Hear, and your soul shall live" (Isaiah 55:3). Who in your sphere of influence needs to hear the salvation message? What if one of the people you come alongside becomes the leader of God's next great movement? Whatever your age, as you yield yourself to do this God-given task, praying for His leadership and guidance along the way, may you do so for His glory!

Ultimately, becoming a leader who raises up other leaders through the process of discipleship requires an investment of time and energy in the spiritual growth of another person. Whether you are confident in your ability, experienced in your approach, or trembling at the prospect of what lies ahead, know that you are already obeying as you strive to let your "conduct be worthy of the gospel of Christ"

> What are you doing to be sure you are trained and able to do what Jesus commands—to both share the gospel and enable others to share the gospel? >

(Philippians 1:27). And this pursuit to honor God by the way you live involves heeding His command to make disciples.

Who is God calling you to raise up in the faith? Choose to cooperate with God's plans to continue to grow you—*and* choose to obey His commands, including the Great Commission, to share the good news of Jesus with others.

Answering God's Callings

BRENT CROWE
Student Leadership University, Orlando, FL

What is God's calling on my life? This is an important and often-asked question. Sadly, the common concern is that an incorrect answer to this question could have significant negative consequences on a person's life. Let me assure you, though, that God is not playing a game of hide-and-seek with our callings, nor is He holding His breath and hoping you figure out the code that opens the door to the room where your calling is waiting to be discovered. You do have a role to play, but as you play that role, remember that God is not hiding His calling on your life from you. That said, I would like to offer some ideas that will help you determine that call:

KNOWING GOD'S CALLING BEGINS WITH UNDERSTANDING THE IMPORTANCE OF "THE PRIESTHOOD OF ALL BELIEVERS."

First Peter 2:9 declares, "You are a chosen race, a royal priesthood, a holy nation, a people for his own possession, that you may proclaim the excellencies of him who called you out of darkness and into his marvelous light" (ESV). This one idea informs virtually every aspect of the Christian life and enables us to understand our relationship with God, our status because of His love, our responsibilities in His mission, and our worship in His presence.

Calling or, in Latin, *vocation* refers to a believer's role in the workplace, society, and the family. During the Reformation, much attention was given to this doctrine, and central to the reformers' message was the notion of "the priesthood of all believers." In his book *God at Work*, Gene Edward Veith makes this important statement: "'The priesthood of all believers' did not make everyone into the church workers; rather, it turned every kind of work into a sacred calling."[1]

THE "PRIESTHOOD OF ALL BELIEVERS" CLEARLY IMPLIES THAT ALL CALLINGS ARE EQUAL.

Central to understanding the doctrine of vocation is the idea that God dwells within us. If we don't believe that—if we live as if God is removed from the everyday world—we are compartmentalizing Him. Francis Schaeffer referred to this as Christianity becoming an "upper story." Yet the truth that God dwells within us logically leads to the truth that God works through people; that, in fact, people are the primary means by which God operates in this world. When we have a proper understanding of *calling* and the doctrine of vocation, we see that all vocations are equally important. Veith said it this way: "This is why all vocations are equal before God. Pastors, monks, nuns, and popes are no holier than farmers, shopkeepers, dairy maids, or latrine diggers."[2]

> *Calling* or, in Latin, *vocation* refers to a believer's role in the workplace, society, and the family. **>**

CALLING IS TO BE UNDERSTOOD AS PLURAL, NOT SINGULAR.

Answering God's call should never be reduced to simply answering the question "What's going to be my job?" Rather, God's call on our lives is fourfold: church, family, citizen, and vocation—and we must guard against elevating one aspect of our calling above another. We must see our calling in the following light: *I am called to Christ and thus to be a part of His church, part of a family, a citizen who cares about the glory of God in the public square, and a contributor to the betterment of society.*

Having considered these three points, you are better prepared to thoughtfully and prayerfully deal with the following action points:

* What gifts, talents, and passions has God given you?
* Which of your gifts or talents do you most enjoy using?

* How can you use that/those gift(s) for the glory of God . . . that is to contribute to the movement of Christianity and the building up of His church?
* How would you use your gifts and talents if you knew you would not fail?
* What can you do now in light of your answer to the previous question?
* Name some individuals who are using a similar gift set in their vocation. If possible, seek them out for wisdom, insight, counsel, and, ideally, a long-term mentoring relationship with them.
* Create a plan that involves attainable goals and then begin working that plan.

I hope you understand both the theological and practical value of the idea of God's calling on your life. Your path may involve trial and error, but be assured that "error" is not necessarily sinful. In other words, I encourage you to try something for the glory of God. "Failing" may be part of your journey toward a more complete understanding of your calling. Failure is the under-rated faculty member in the curriculum of our lives. Those who never fail are probably those who never dared to dream and imagine what could be, no matter the odds.

In the end, gaining an understanding of your callings is a journey in itself. And during that journey you will most certainly find your patience tested, your identity in Christ strengthened, and your vision of what God wants for your life clarified.

Making an Impact
Right Where You Are

KEN BURNETT
Fellowship of Christian Athletes, Huntsville, AL

Have you ever been driving along and just sensed you were going the wrong direction? Maybe you weren't even driving. Maybe you were riding shotgun, and something didn't feel right. Well, that's exactly the feeling I had when I was driving late one night. I had actually gotten a little sleepy, so I'd pulled over at a gas station to get a snack and wake up a bit.

After returning to the car with my ice cream, I pulled onto the highway and immediately had this weird feeling. *Did I forget something at the gas station? Did I leave my wallet on the counter? Or my drink on top of the car—again?* Nope. I hadn't taken anything into the store, so I couldn't have left my wallet. And I hadn't bought a drink, so that wasn't it either. I had my cruise control on, so I knew I wasn't speeding. But something was different.

As I drove farther down the road, I actually began to have a mini panic attack. Again, I knew I wasn't speeding because I had my cruise control on. But just to be sure I decided to check the next speed limit sign—and there it was. The problem, though, was not the *number* on the speed limit sign. The problem was the *location* of the sign. It was so far off the road that even with my lights, I couldn't see the number.

BAM! It hit me. I suddenly knew what was wrong. *I am on the wrong side of the four-lane highway!* When I'd pulled back onto the road, I'd been so focused on my ice cream that I drove onto the wrong side of the highway. The reality of my mistake hit hard as two bright lights came over the hill and headed toward me. I couldn't scream because my wife was asleep during all this craziness. Looking to the right, I considered crossing the median. The hazard of the unknown made me decide against that option. So, starting to sweat, I did the unthinkable, the craziest thing I could have done! I sped up!

I sped up to beat the oncoming car. I started driving faster toward the car that was coming toward me. Yes! I know! I was insane! Yet in the moment I just wanted to find a safe way to cross to the other side of the highway. Definitely not the best idea! So what should I have done? What would you have done?

In the midst of the excitement, my wife woke up. She later told me she could tell by the sweat on my face that something was wrong. She usually sees me enjoying ice cream in a more chilled-out way . . .

I have written many special quotes inside my favorite book in the world . . . my Bible. Here is one of them: "You can impress people from a distance, but you impact them up close." I have had the pleasure of serving students for over twenty years. Through the years many students and adults have told me how badly they wanted to make an impact! With tears, they have shared how much they wanted to change their campus or change this world for Jesus Christ. I get so excited to hear them talk, but time and time again these well-meaning students try to have an impact all too quickly or by impressing people. This approach leads to little or no impact.

All I had to do on the road that night to be safe when I was going the wrong way was to stop and turn **The Bible is a great book of God-given, time-tested advice.** around. Then I would have been going the right way, I would have been safer faster, and I would have enjoyed my ice cream a whole lot more!

The Bible has a powerful verse in the book of Proverbs: "The way of a fool seems right to him, but a wise man listens to advice" (12:15 NIV).

Friend, you are growing up in the most informed generation ever to exist in the human race, but at times you and your friends go so fast to get to a better way (like my trying to get to the median) that you don't listen to advice. Well, the Bible is a great book of God-given, time-tested advice. It begs us to listen and be wise; it warns us that not to listen is to be a fool. I pray today that you will choose to be wise, heed the Bible's advice, and start impacting others for Christ:

> Love must be sincere. Hate what is evil; cling to what is good. Be devoted to one another in brotherly love. Honor one another above yourselves. Never be lacking in zeal, but keep your spiritual fervor, serving the Lord. Be joyful in hope, patient in affliction, faithful in prayer. Share with God's people who are in need. Practice hospitality.

> Bless those who persecute you; bless and do not curse. Rejoice with those who rejoice; mourn with those who mourn. Live in harmony with one another. Do not be proud, but be willing to associate with people of low position. Do not be conceited.

> Do not repay anyone evil for evil. Be careful to do what is right in the eyes of everybody. If it is possible, as far as it depends on you, live at peace with everyone. (Romans 12:9–18 NIV)

Missions—for Life!

CHRISTIAN NICHLES
First Baptist Church Midland, Midland, TX

"If anyone desires to come after Me,
let him deny himself, and take up his cross daily, and follow Me."

—JESUS IN LUKE 9:23

We step off the plane, the team hugs one final time, we pray that the work that was done will continue to bless, all say their good-byes, and everyone goes home.

That single sentence probably describes the final scene of many spring-break and summertime mission trips, those wonderful, life-transforming trips that we will never forget. However, after the highlight video has been played at church and the participants have given a testimony about all God did, it's over. We move on to the next event, on to the next trip, all the while moving further and further away from the very life that God has called us to live, a life of fulfillment because we aware of His presence with us and His power at work in us and through us. Why is it that, while we're on mission trips, service projects, and outreaches, we feel close to God, fulfilled, and completely powerful—and we don't at home?

That question calls forth another question: "Why am I not serving, giving, and sacrificing every day the way I did for [insert name of trip or outreach]?" After seeing Christ work in a mighty way, we can find it a real downer to leave the site of that amazing moment and go back to the "real" world. So why don't we live so that we experience such moments even when we're home and back in our routine?

To answer that question, let's take a moment to examine some basic principles that may help us all live missionally every day, not just on church trips or service projects. First, to prepare for a mission outreach, someone identifies a need that must be met and then makes plans to meet that need in the best way possible. Second, the need is presented, God touches people's hearts, moving them to get involved, and the team is assembled. Third, this team begins to meet regularly to pray, asking God to bless their efforts and to provide strength for what they will encounter. Fourth, each team member sacrifices a week or two of their time, not to mention lots of money, in order to go and meet this need. Last, they are obedient in their going and their serving well. They encounter the Lord like never before as they meet the needs of those they've prayed and prepared for—and they inevitably come home changed.

Now, imagine prepping for every day the way you prep for a mission trip. That's right. What if every day of your life you awakened to the idea that you have been called to go to a place with real needs (your school, a sports team, your afternoon job, band, etc.) and to meet the needs of those you encounter? What if every day you took a minute or two to meet a solitary someone with a smile or a kind word? Or maybe you decide that not another person in the cafeteria will have to eat lunch alone again? What if, in every moment of every day, you prayed and asked God to prepare you for the people and situations you will encounter throughout that day? What if you were then bold enough to stand in these everyday areas and invite others to join you to meet these needs? I'll tell you what would happen: that same spiritual fire you felt when you stepped off that airplane would be upon you every day. That same sense of kingdom accomplishment and fulfillment would fill you daily. The same great wave of God's mercy and grace that you saw flow into the hearts of those orphans when you loved them will be multiplied each day as the—figuratively speaking—orphans at your school

> **No matter where you go, you can be on a mission! >**

and in your community become God's adopted sons and daughters. Finally, you will see that you're not alone. Jesus has invited others to join you on a similar mission. As you obediently follow Jesus into the mission field of your daily life at home, you will encounter opportunities to do what you were created to do: share God's love and His gospel truth.

You only have one shot at this life, and you will only be truly fulfilled when you accomplish the mission God created you to do, and that mission certainly calls for more than just one or two weeks out of every year. So will you be a catalyst of change in your school, on your team, at your church, or in your community? The challenge lies now in responding to the call. Just as you sign up for that trip and pay that deposit, as a Christ follower you signed up for this. When you named Jesus as your Savior and Lord, you agreed to be on a lifelong mission with Him, not just occasionally take a trip. It's the abandoning of one's self and relying on God's provision that makes a mission trip so powerful. It's no different in our daily life.

So today, will you prepare yourself to live on a mission? Will you be prayerful, sensitive to the needs of those around you, and willing to help? Will you sound the call and assemble a team to serve? Will you sacrifice time and resources to serve God and people? This is the only way missions will be your life and not just another trip. No matter where you go, you can be on a mission! Remember that Jesus called His followers—then and now—to "be witnesses to Me in Jerusalem, and in all Judea and Samaria, and to the end of the earth" (Acts 1:8).

Now . . . GO!

Live a Life of Mission

MATT PETTY
Burnt Hickory Baptist Church, Powder Springs, GA

I believe with all my heart that God did not design our bodies to remain motionless or in one place for any length of time. Instead, I believe that God designed each one of us to be active for His glory. We were made to be the hands and feet of Jesus to everyone we meet. Some of the most amazing people I've met are those who have found what God would have them do and are right in the middle of doing exactly that.

Have you ever been just a bit jealous of those people? Have you ever wondered how they heard from the Lord what they were specifically created to do? The sad reality is that a large portion of us believers will use the "let's just sit and wait" approach to finding our callings. While it may seem like a great plan to wait for the Lord's handwriting to appear on the wall, I'm not sure that's God's plan. Let me give you another option: Go and do *something*!

If Jesus is your King, then—in His power—you are old enough, good enough, and strong enough to be God's servant. In fact, He has already called you to be exactly that. But we have turned God's will for our lives into this mystical feeling or a hard-to-find direction. Too many of us—young people and adults alike—give up trying to find out, much less live out, God's calling. That's why I believe God most often solidifies a specific calling when we are in the middle of doing something for Him. Think about it. What if the disciples had never taken a chance and just up and followed Jesus? What if young David had never stepped up to face the giant on the battlefield? Many pastors and missionaries today started with an attitude of "Let's go live a life of mission and see what happens!" The funny thing is . . . God takes care of the rest. He will call some to be pastors, moms, missionaries, cashiers, teachers, church planters, plumbers, youth pastors, businesspeople, cooks, doctors . . . The list goes on.

There is no limit to the mission opportunities God can put in front of us. So the issue we must respond to is, "What kinds of situations do I need to put myself in to allow God to move in me on a specific path? What do I need to experience to see where I fit?" And here's a tool to help you come up with answers to those questions. Look at the categories of missionary opportunities below—and then go and do!

> Go and do *something*! >

1. **Your community:** Many of us overlook the hurts and needs of people in our own backyard when we think of missions. But what if, for the next six months, we all regularly sought to meet a need we pass by every day? We would be amazed by the number of opportunities all around us that we could address without even packing a bag. And what might happen if you took a week off of life and did a mission trip at home? You never know! You just may find your passion right in your own backyard.

2. **A place ripe for the gospel:** I'm talking about a location somewhere around the globe that God is blessing, some place where people are coming to know Jesus, a place begging for willing folks to step into and let God shine. You may find that your mission in life is to be planted in a slum or a third-world country where God is clearly moving.

3. **An urban setting:** Life in major cities is different from life in other places. (Urban life is faster, and people's lifestyles are impacted by that reality.) Most church-planting strategists say that we believers must reach the urban centers around the globe if the world is to hear the gospel. For that work, God needs many people doing a variety of things,

including running a coffeehouse, managing a soup kitchen, planting a church, teaching at an inner city school, or being a social worker on the frontlines. An urban setting can introduce you to many missionary options and help you determine whether your heart is drawn to one.

4. **A place that is either pre- or post-Christian:** This category includes places where the vast majority of Christians have died or been run out, as well as places that have never been reached with the gospel. Creative ways to slowly introduce the gospel are basic requirements. We must earn people's trust in order to share Jesus. While places where the gospel is ripe see thousands come to Christ, this type of ministry starts with something as small as sharing a meal with a neighbor.

5. **A needy place:** You and I are blessed far beyond what we deserve. That's why nothing can substitute our experiencing a place of genuine poverty with its smells, sights, feelings, and conversations. Only when you are among people who truly do depend on God for today's bread will you develop a real heart for the starving, hurting, needy world that's out there. In fact, it's in the middle of some of the toughest, most heartbreaking places on earth that God often clarifies life callings.

I realize that it may be hard, if not impossible, to experience missions in every category listed. But living a life of mission is not about checking off all the categories. The point is to get somewhere and listen for God to speak to you. Remember, missions is 50 percent doing and 50 percent God teaching us who He wants us to be. So don't just sit at home and hope He shows you. Go and do!

Needed: World-Class Change Agents

ROGER GLIDEWELL
Global Youth Ministry, Chatsworth, GA

o you want to change your world? I truly hope so because our world desperately needs help!

Around the globe, your fellow youth suffer greatly because of the growing epidemic of issues that affect them: the breakdown of the family, poor education, environmental pollution, poverty, sex trafficking, abortion, drug abuse, suicide, and more. Far worse than these societal injustices is the reality that millions of youth worldwide are slipping into eternity without Christ. Clearly, world-class change agents are needed to bring fresh hope to our fallen world. And before you decide you can't do anything to help your generation, let me— with some encouragement from Nehemiah—point out three things you can do to become a world-class change agent in your world.

CHANGE YOUR MIND . . . FROM NEGATIVE TO POSITIVE!

Where does a young person like you go to begin to change things that are far bigger than you are? Obviously, you need to access a source of greater power. In Nehemiah's day, the people of God were captives in a foreign land. Nehemiah himself was a slave, serving as cupbearer to the king. (Job description: Cupbearer drinks the Kool-Aid before giving it to the king to see if it was poisoned! Talk about expendable!) But when Nehemiah heard about the terrible plight of the people of Jerusalem, he took the problem straight to the king. No, not to King Artaxerxes, but to the King of kings!

Instead of caving to negativity, Nehemiah sought positive change at the seat of all power: "I was fasting and praying before the God of heaven" (Nehemiah 1:4). And as he prayed, he asked God to use him to effect change. So . . . what happened? The pagan King Artaxerxes was moved to help Nehemiah accomplish a God-sized task!

> The Holy Spirit first produces change *in* us before He ignites transforming change *through* us to impact our world. **>**

God changes entire cultures by first changing our own minds and hearts. Romans 12:2 says, "Be transformed by the renewing of your mind." The Holy Spirit first produces change *in* us before He ignites transforming change *through* us to impact our world. Set change in motion by praying that God will change *your mind* to believe that "nothing is impossible with God" (Luke 1:37 NIV).

CHANGE YOUR MEANS . . . FROM EXTERNAL TO INTERNAL!

Many policymakers, news commentators, and others have advocated government mandates and court intervention as the means to engineer massive societal change. Nehemiah had the necessary governmental authority to make changes, but he also needed volunteers to actually build the wall. Nehemiah started a chain reaction in which many people *volunteered* to rebuild the walls of Jerusalem. How did he do this? Impose martial law? No! Nehemiah 2:12 explains that he started this process by instilling hope in "a few men" who got it!

Huge change often begins small, starting with *internal* motivation rather than *external* laws. The Holy Spirit is the consummate change agent who transforms people from the inside out. Lives are mended; broken marriages are restored; neighborhoods are reclaimed from drugs and poverty one person at a time. John Newton, who wrote the enduring hymn "Amazing Grace," was a transformed slave trader. William Wilberforce launched a campaign in Parliament to abolish slave trade in the British Empire after he was first converted to faith in Christ. John Wesley turned to Christ as a youth and started a religious club on campus . . . out of which grew the Methodist Church!

By what means do we impact society? Simple: we share the gospel of Jesus Christ with people one by one. Your personal witness can be the powerful instrument that God uses to start a tidal wave of positive change. As believers, we must *never* trade church programs or government policies for the transformative power of the Holy Spirit who is able to ignite internal (and eternal) change in individuals—change that then impacts families, communities, even countries!

You don't have to wait until you get a college education to share Christ. You don't have to get a full-time job. You don't have to be elected to public office. While these approaches may

> By what means do we impact society? Simple: we share the gospel of Jesus Christ with people one by one. >

be helpful, none of them are *essential* for you to become a powerful change agent *today* through your persuasive witness.

CHANGE YOUR MISSION . . . FROM "ONLY HERE" TO ANYWHERE!

Right now over 50 percent of the earth's population is aged twenty-nine and under. Tragically, most of the 2 billion young people on this planet live without hope in Christ and are headed for hell. Approximately 95 percent of all resources being used on earth to reach youth with the gospel are spent on American teenagers. That leaves only 5 percent of youth ministry resources to reach 95 percent of the world's youth with the gospel. You can change that: you can personally bring the gospel to your peers! "Oh," you protest, "I could never raise funds or leave my country to minister to lost youth in Africa or Asia or wherever. I'll just witness right here and leave those youth to missionaries."

Really?

Nehemiah learned about terrible problems in a faraway place. He was a slave, separated from the situation by hundreds of miles. How ridiculous for him to think he could be released from bondage, acquire massive resources, and cross hundreds of miles of extremely dangerous terrain to personally improve the situation of people far away in Jerusalem!

Nevertheless, Nehemiah saw himself as part of the solution. He overcame herculean problems to personally go to Jerusalem to help change the equation there: "Then I went to the governors in the region beyond the River" (Nehemiah 2:9). Wow, so much for our excuses! We aren't slaves like Nehemiah. But when he, a slave, made himself available to God, amazing things began to happen. Are you available?

Just as Nehemiah became a world-class change agent, so can you. The key question is, "Will you?" Start by changing your *mind* (by positive prayer), your *means* (seek individual transformation), and your *mission* (go anywhere God leads)! Be the world-class change agent your generation needs—and start now!

Living Out Your Faith

> WILL HAGLE
> Mobberly Baptist Church, Longview, TX

I t's a three-step process, but maybe one you haven't thought much about. I'm talking about spiritual growth and the cycle of Discovery ➥ Ownership ➥ Leadership. Here are some details.

1. *Discovery* is the very first step toward knowing the things of God. Listening to a sermon, attending a small group, reading the Bible—these are avenues of discovery. And I'd say we have this down pretty well. You probably have no problem finding opportunities to discover spiritual things.

2. After we discover a spiritual principle, the next step is *ownership*. (I encourage you to read about ownership on page 155 before you read this section). Don't lead—don't attempt to lead—based on truths that you are not taking ownership of in your heart. (That lack of conviction weakens truth to mere ideas.) If you do not own a truth, you are not ready to lead, model, teach, or be an example of it. Ownership provides the motivation for leadership: "In your hearts honor Christ the Lord as holy, always being prepared to make a defense to anyone who asks you for a reason for the hope that is in you" (1 Peter 3:15 ESV). Notice that ownership comes first: "In your hearts." Spiritual ownership is embracing as truly your own every aspect of your relationship with God and every truth about Him that you discover. Once you discover a spiritual principle and take ownership of it, then you should exercise spiritual leadership.

3. Spiritual leadership basically means living out your faith in front of other people. The world needs real examples of authentic Christlike living. And when you live your faith, people in your sphere of influence notice. No matter your age or position, you have an opportunity to let others see Jesus in you. Spiritual leadership is all about using your influence with others as you live life God's way. God wants to use you right where you are. You

can impact for Christ every single person you come in contact with: family, friends, acquaintances, strangers, even enemies. You influence others when you reflect Christ's character and values: when you serve them, love them, encourage them; when you share the gospel with them; and so on.

Now consider how the greatest two commandments give us an example of how this cycle leads us to leadership. Jesus shared the greatest commandment in Matthew 22:37: "Love the LORD your God with all your heart, with all your soul, and with all your mind." Clearly, we are to love God with our whole being, and we must love God more than we love anyone or anything else. Jesus shared the second greatest commandment two verses later: "Love your neighbor as yourself." After you *discover* these truths, you must *own* them. You must sincerely accept them. Then you should *live* them out. You should take action. You should live your life actually loving God more than you love anything else. Look for real ways to love others. As you live out your love for God and for others, people around you will notice. And that is spiritual leadership.

> When you live your faith, people in your sphere of influence notice. >

But when we hear the word *leader*, many of us think of the person in charge, the person in front showing the rest what to do and where to go. Leaders in our culture are the successful and talented people, the people with the best personality, or the most qualified people. And leaders are served by others. In the Bible, however, we find a very different picture of a *leader*. We find that the first shall be last and the last shall be first (Mark 10:31). We find servants (Mark 10:43). We find unqualified and imperfect people being used mightily by God. And He used them because they trusted Him, sought His will, and lived it.

So where are you in the Discovery ☞ Ownership ☞ Leadership cycle? A number of signs indicate when a student is figuring out what spiritual leadership is: inviting friends to church, seeking to honor parents in a culture where many students do not, showing a love and concern for others, placing others first, telling people about Jesus, looking for every opportunity to encourage others, making sacrifices, living by the Spirit, deciding to "be an example to the believers in word, in conduct, in love, in spirit, in faith, in purity" (1 Timothy 4:12). Do you see any evidence of spiritual leadership in your life?

And why is spiritual leadership a critical issue for today's young people? I can think of some very good reasons. Statistics show that students are presently leaving the church in droves after they graduate from high school. This country desperately needs examples of authentic believers your age living out their faith. The future will need leaders as well, and you are the leaders of tomorrow. But, even more importantly, spiritual leadership is God's plan. God wants every child of His to impact others:

> You are the light of the world. A city that is set on a hill cannot be hidden. Nor do they light a lamp and put it under a basket, but on a lampstand, and it gives light to all who are in the house. Let your light so shine before men, that they may see your good works and glorify your Father in heaven. (Jesus in Matthew 5:14–16)

Notice that the lamp gives light to everyone around. Similarly, you have the opportunity to influence every single person around you in every situation. So live for the Lord, lead according to in His commands, and be the light of the world!

Jesus Chose Who?

CHRIS WHITE
Mobilizing Students, Fayetteville, GA

When I was in seminary, I learned—and remembered—something very interesting from Dr. Roy Fish in my evangelism classes. Did you know that every major spiritual awakening in the history of the world—from Pentecost to the Reformation, to the First, Second, and Third Great Awakenings here in the United States, and including the Jesus Movement of the 1970s—began with teenagers and college students? Furthermore, statistics also show that 85 percent of the people who come to faith in Christ do so before the age of eighteen.

Not only did both of those facts stun me, but they intrigued to me. So I began to wonder, *If all the major spiritual awakenings throughout history began with students, and if the bulk of people who surrender their lives to Christ are students, then what does the Bible say about teenagers? How are they represented in Scripture?* So I began digging through Scripture, Jewish history, and information about ancient cultures. I want to share a very important discovery.

An interesting detail in history suggests that of the twelve disciples Jesus chose, eleven of them may have been teenagers; possibly only one of them—Peter—was an adult. Could that be true? How do we even know that? Matthew 17:24–27 offers a detail that may be significant:

> When they had come to Capernaum, those who received the temple tax came to Peter and said, "Does your Teacher not pay the temple tax?" He said, "Yes." And when he had come into the house, Jesus anticipated him, saying, "What do you think, Simon? From whom do the kings of the earth take customs or taxes, from their sons or from strangers?" Peter said to Him, "From strangers." Jesus said to him, "Then the sons are free. Nevertheless, lest we offend them, go to the sea, cast in a hook, and take the fish that comes up first. And when you have

opened its mouth, you will find a piece of money; take that and give it to them for Me and you."

The key detail is "give [the tax] . . . for Me and you." According to Jewish law, anyone twenty years old or older was required to pay the temple tax, and apparently only Jesus and Peter paid it. Maybe the two of them were the only to pay because that is who "those who received the temple tax" approached. But maybe only Jesus and Peter paid the tax because they were the only ones in the group of disciples who were older than twenty years of age. That suggests that Jesus chose eleven teenagers and one adult as His disciples, His replacements, His apostles, the ones entrusted to take the gospel to every nation, tribe, and tongue. That makes Jesus the greatest student pastor in the world!

This detail may also suggest why Peter was probably the spokesperson for the disciples every time they were questioned. Of course, when he proclaimed that Jesus is "the Christ, the Son of the living God" (Matthew 16:16), Jesus commended him and declared that this truth would be the rock for the church, but perhaps another reason Jesus made Peter a leader was his status as the oldest. Peter stood up and proclaimed the gospel at Pentecost. He was the one who defended the claims of Christ before the Sanhedrin (Acts 4). He led the way during the first eight chapters of Acts and became a pillar—a rock—of faith for the early believers. Isn't that crazy? Isn't that awesome? If teenagers numbered among Jesus' inner circle, then why are we in the church today babysitting you and treating you like overgrown children even when you're in your midtwenties?

Let me remind us that, ironically, we send our seventeen- and eighteen-year-olds to fight our wars, the average age of Joseph Kony's LRA (Lord's Resistance Army) in Africa was fourteen, and David was around age fourteen when he slew Goliath—and he'd already killed a lion and a bear. In our modern era, seventh-grader Zac Hunter wrote a book called *Be the Change* in his effort to alleviate slavery among the 27 million slaves worldwide. Throughout history, most of the great achievements in the fields of art, culture, science, and technology have been by teenagers.[1]

Also remember that Mary was a teenager when the angel Gabriel appeared to her and told her that she would be the mother of the long-awaited Messiah.

> Young people are far more capable of doing great things for the glory of God than we allow you to do. >

It is time for the church to understand the incredible value that you young people bring to the body of Christ. You are far more capable of doing great things for the glory of God than we allow you to do. Since Jesus apparently chose teenagers, we in the twenty-first-century church should do the same!

Almighty God, I know You have incredible plans for me. Not just down the road, but right now. I want my life to count for Your kingdom. Please show me the steps I need to take to be engaged in taking the gospel to the nations right now, while I'm a teenager. I will follow You wherever You lead. In Jesus' name, amen.

Coaching and Being Coached

CHUCK ALLEN
Sugar Hill Church, Sugar Hill, GA

[Jesus] went up on the mountain and called to Him those He Himself wanted. And they came to Him. Then He appointed twelve, that they might be with Him and that He might send them out to preach.

—MARK 3:13–14

Has it ever occurred to you that nothing has ever just occurred to God? Think about it. God has never once walked through the hallways of heaven and thought, *Well, how about that!* Every minute—every nanosecond—of every day God has this unique and wonderful plan for you to wildly succeed at being the person He wants you to be. That includes who He puts in your path to help you achieve that success.

Mark 3:13–14 gives us a peek into the simple, yet powerful way that Jesus coached those around Him. Jesus chose the Twelve to "be with Him" that they might learn from Him. Jesus called these disciples to watch Him model godliness and teach them servant leadership before He sent them out to change the world forever. Jesus also coached the members of His team so they could one day coach others. He modeled for them what life is really all about and then sent them out to succeed. That's what a good mentor, a good coach, does.

I learned the value of being coached when I played football. My coaches learned who I really was and who I could be, and they knew when to get in my face and when to encourage me. You see, they knew and I knew that I needed a coach if I was to be the best player I could be. So it is in our walk with Christ: each of us needs godly men and women to invest in our lives so that we can reach our God-given potential. Maybe you are wondering what a coach would do for you. A good coach will help you discover what you do well, where your blind spots are, and how you can accomplish all God has planned for you to accomplish. A good coach, then, sounds like someone we all need.

But—I know what you're thinking—*do I really need a coach? I've got this, right?* No! You don't, and neither does anyone else. The concept of a self-made man is a myth. God has built us in such a way that we need help each and every day. You were created with amazing strengths, and you undoubtedly face some very real challenges. A coach can help you craft your strengths and overcome your challenges. And of course the person you select as your mentor will have a huge impact on who you become.

So what kind of person should you ask to be your coach?

> A coach can help you craft your strengths and overcome your challenges. >

FIND A GREAT LEADER

Look for a leader whom God has stamped with His seal of approval—"Servant Leader." After all, Jesus Himself said, "Whoever desires to become great among you shall be your servant" (Mark 10:43). So look for someone who is a great leader in God's eyes. A servant who is there to help you succeed, not use you so that he or she can look good. A servant who is willing to set aside personal gain and glory in order to help you become the person God has planned you to be.

FIND SOMEONE WHO WILL NEVER LET YOU STOP LEARNING

A coach will always challenge you to learn, to grow, to be stretched, to challenge yourself to *be* more, *do* more, and *excel*. Being able to hear and respond to those challenges requires you to recognize that you don't know everything about everything. It requires that you want to better yourself by learning from those around you. It requires your willingness to be both transparent with your coach and accountable to him or her. Great leaders are always willing to be held accountable. They know that the more they learn, the better they'll do. That's why we need coaches who push us to learn and then hold us accountable to live out those lessons.

CHARACTER IS KEY

In the same way that you look to be coached, look to be willing to coach. After all, just like you, everyone else in God's wonderful creation has amazing strengths and faces certain challenges. They need to be coached as well. But both finding a great coach and being a great coach requires something special, something called *character*. When artists start in on a new canvas, it's impossible to tell their intentions for the painting after seeing only a few strokes of the brush. But eventually, stroke by stroke, the painting is created and the artist's intention is revealed. In the same way, your character—who you really are inside—is slowly revealed over time, decision by decision, choice by choice. Every reaction to every life circumstance is another stroke of the brush on your self-portrait. Your character is revealed in your actions and reactions. And to some degree you choose your character—you choose who you are—by choosing who coaches you and, at some point, how you coach!

Your willingness to be mentored or coached reveals much about your character—and it's totally your choice. Choosing to be coached improves the odds that you will leave an imprint of excellence on this planet. Or you can choose mediocrity. It's all about growing in Christ.

The Power of Humility

RON LUCE
Teen Mania, Garden Valley, TX

ou know that fake humility, don't you? It says, "I'm really a nothing," but inside it's conceited and arrogant. That's not what God wants. And neither does He want you to believe that you are nothing. That's not humility either.

Genuine humility recognizes who God is in all His glory, who you are in your sinfulness, and the fact that God loves you anyway. You are the apple of God's eye (Zechariah 2:8), and He declares you beautifully and wonderfully made (Psalm 139:14). And God promises that if you humble yourself in a right relationship with Him, recognizing that He is the Lord and you are His servant, He will lift you up (James 4:10).

Jesus Himself came to this earth in meekness and humility as a servant. Don't misunderstand this to mean Jesus was weak. Remember when He threw all the moneychangers out of the temple? Remember how He thundered when He preached to the religious leaders about their hypocrisy? Jesus was no wimp.

And rather than meaning "weak," *meek* means "controlled power." This person—think *Jesus*—knows he has power and knows he is strong, but he controls his strength. He *chooses* to be humble instead of flaunting or bragging about his abilities. Jesus was the most powerful human being to ever walk this earth, yet He described Himself as "gentle and humble in heart" (Matthew 11:29 NIV). He loved people and poured out His compassion on them. He wasn't puffed up or always trying to put Himself above others. In fact, Jesus washed His disciples' feet (John 13). He came to serve (Matthew 20:28). He had nothing to prove to anyone. Jesus knew He was the Son of God, and He rested in that solid sense of identity and purpose. And when Jesus exercised His divine strength, it was clearly controlled power.

God is looking for people today who have controlled power. That is meek-ness: people who know who they are, who know the strength they have in God, and who refuse to back down. Yet when you look in the faces of these people, you will

> Genuine humility recognizes who God is in all His glory, who you are in your sinfulness, and the fact that God loves you anyway. >

see humility and gentleness. These people know that a servant's attitude is what reaches other people. No wonder Jesus taught, "Blessed are the meek" (Matthew 5:5).

Jesus is the best example of controlled strength. He showed us the kind of strength that comes from being humble and serving others. Too many people today believe putting others before yourself or willingly submitting to author-ity is a sign of weakness. Our culture says, "Be your own person! Don't let anyone tell you what to do. Do what *you* want!"

But Jesus sees strength in humility. The more humble you are, in fact, the stronger you are. (You, for instance, will not succumb to peer pressure.) Humility is also evident when you serve other people. In contrast, arrogant people don't have time to meet anyone's needs or even have time to listen to them. Arrogance makes us think we are too important to slow down and care. It also makes us very concerned about our reputation.

Humility is knowing that in Christ you are strong. You don't find it intimi-dating to slow down and spend time with people, even people who aren't popular. You're learning something else that Jesus modeled: He never cared what people thought of Him.

So the Bible commands us to be humble. Here's a how-to tip: the key to remaining humble is casting all of your cares on God (1 Peter 5:6–7). By laying all your worries at God's feet, you are saying, "Lord, I can't do this without You. I need Your help."

And here's a second how-to: it's pretty easy to be genuinely humble if you continually see yourself as a servant. You're not here to be in charge or tell people what to do. You're here to serve. Decide every morning to walk into the day with a servant's heart.

We may think that if we're going to be humble, we have to be poor and have nothing—and that doesn't appeal to the average affluent American. But Scripture shows that the very opposite is true. When God sees your humble heart, He will bless you.

In James 4:6, however, we read that "God resists the proud, but gives grace to the humble." God opposes the proud. Sadly, a lot of Christians are prideful because of what they own, what they do for a living, or even because they behave "better" than others. Yet God opposes these people.

Choose to be a servant. >

And God gives grace to the humble. God wants us to be people of humility, and our humility should be evident in all areas of our lives—our friendships as well as our relationships with our parents, our pastors, our employers, and our coworkers. Be radically committed to being a humble servant in every aspect of your life. Even though you know who you are in Christ—a strong child of God, who has the all-powerful Holy Spirit living within you—choose to be a servant. And choose to be respectful and act humbly in the face of authority. This might mean you need to apologize to your parents, teachers, boss, or other authority figure for any arrogance you've exhibited toward them.

"Clothe [yourself] with humility" in all areas (1 Peter 5:5 NIV). Whenever you are tempted to prove you are right, choose a gentle answer and turn away wrath instead (Proverbs 15:1). Living in humility like that, you will reflect the life of the Lord and draw more people to Him.

Lord Jesus, I humble myself before You, acknowledging that You are the Son of God and that You have saved me. Please let me be one of Your meek, humble followers who serves selflessly. Use me to give You glory and draw people to You. Humility doesn't come naturally, but I will choose to put on a humble attitude. Give me opportunities to serve people. In Jesus' name, amen.

#communicating

Using Your Influence for Good

BRAD HOBBS
Student Leadership University, Orlando, FL

I n 1999, *TIME* magazine faced a question that no magazine or print publication in the history of the world had ever faced: "Who was the most important person of the millennium?" This span of time had seen people like Christopher Columbus, Martin Luther, Michelangelo, Isaac Newton, George Washington, and Mother Teresa—and *TIME* was asking who was the most significant?

In answer to its own question, *TIME* looked to the fifteenth-century and a man by the name of Johannes Gutenberg. Between 1454 and 1455, Gutenberg developed the ability to mass-produce print publications so that the average person could own books. The printing press also meant that men and women could enhance their knowledge through personal reading and not just by listening to what the local scholar or priest said.

Before Gutenberg, only 80 percent of the world could even write their own name, much less read a book.[1] Gutenberg's press transformed everything— and presented the leaders of society with a very great challenge: How could this new invention be used for the greatest good?

Once the printing press began to circulate information, men and women from around the world could learn for themselves and gain knowledge from books, magazines, journals, and eventually the Internet. The invention of social media, however, has flipped the history of information and ideas on its head. With social media, you are no longer merely a recipient of information; social media makes you a participant who contributes to the world around you information about life and experiences. Social media now gives you the opportunity to broadcast your life as fast as you can take a picture. For six hundred

  • • • • • • • • • • • • • • • • • •

years, authors and publishers tried to send you information, and now authors and publishers are listening to you through the online avenues of social media.

So the same question raised by the invention of the printing press must be asked of you today: "How do I, as a follower of Christ, use social media and my influence for the most good?" Here are a few thoughts in response to that question:

Know your profile. In social media you can change your profile picture, your information, and the people you want to be associated with, but none of that defines who you are. You were designed in the image of God, and no profile or status can change that. Having been created in God's image means you are designed to reflect His glory and His character with every breath, word, and action. The greatest purpose you have—whether online or in person—is to reflect the endless glory of God as you live for Him and serve Him. This standard is to be the filter for every decision you make in life (Genesis 1:27; 2 Corinthians 3:18; Titus 3:14).

Take an intent look into the future. What would a college, a possible employer, or maybe even your future spouse think about you if they only saw your social media pages? The reality is, whatever you put online now will never be erased. You might delete crude comments or indecent images from your profile, but the Internet stores all those things in the cloud. Google keeps a profile on you, and that profile records everything you ever search for. You are playing games with your future when you refuse to consider the lasting consequences of what you do online or through social media. God has an extraordinary future laid out for you; don't derail it by putting online an immature picture or a thoughtless comment (Proverbs 6:16–23; 2 Timothy 2:22–23).

Take a sabbatical. Social media is so enticing that it often becomes a full-time preoccupation. You need to schedule daily, weekly, and monthly breaks when you shut down all your media and spend quality time thinking about your own spiritual journey, read a challenging book, and interact with your family or close friends. Just as you need a break from school in order to effectively learn, you need a break from the virtual if you are to effectively live in the real. Start this week by scheduling one hour when you won't use anything that has an on/off switch (Psalm 63; Mark 6:31).

Supplement your relationships. Just as a protein shake supplements an athlete's workout, social media can supplement your relationships with the people you interact with. Social media cannot build close friendships just as a protein shake cannot build muscles without physical exercise. So spend face-to-face time with people, hanging out, encouraging, and sharpening one another—and use social media to reinforce those connections. Supplementing your friendships with social media means that what you do online will either strengthen or weaken the relationships you have with close friends. Find a way to encourage your close friends through social media this week (Proverbs 27:17; Romans 12:10; Revelation 12:11).

Be completely transparent—but not online. You were born into a world where people long to live transparently and openly and never be judged for anything we say or do. However, as a Christian, you will give an account for everything you do and say to the Creator of the universe. Therefore, when you get mad, feel deeply hurt, or want to fire off at someone, run to Him instead. Run to the God who created you and share with Him. After all, He not only knows you better than anyone else does, but He also cares more deeply about what you are facing in life. Don't allow social media to be who God longs to be in your life. This week find some quiet time and a quiet place to share with God the things on your heart and mind (Psalm 55:22; Matthew 11:28–30).

As a follower of Christ, choose to use social media and the influence you have through it for good.

Culture and Reality TV

JOSEPH MCMURRY
Carmel Baptist Church, Matthews, NC

Google search of *reality TV* in combination with words like *statistics,* *impact,* or *effects* will uncover a multitude of valuable resources on the topic. Even a casual investigation of the research available shows that reality TV has had and is having a significant effect on students and culture both here in the United States and abroad. Although it was thought to be a temporary phenomenon in response to a television writers strike in 2001, reality TV seems here to stay.

In 2011, the Girl Scout Research Institute surveyed 1,141 girls across the United States between the ages of eleven and seventeen. Everyone surveyed agreed that reality shows promote bad behavior. Eighty-six percent felt that the shows often set girls against one another to make the program more dramatic, and 70 percent believed that reality TV leads viewers to think it's okay to treat people badly.[1]

Statistics released in September of 2011 from the National Center on Addiction and Substance Abuse show that younger kids who watch reality shows like *Jersey Shore* and *16 and Pregnant* are twice as likely to smoke cigarettes and drink and more than one and a half times as likely to smoke marijuana.[2]

One student, whom I asked about the lure of reality TV, told me that he believes the greatest draw of shows like *The Bachelor, Big Brother,* and *Keeping Up with the Kardashians* is pride. He said, "I watch reality shows because they make me feel smarter and better [than the people on the shows]." Such pride is an easy trap for many watchers of reality TV. Social ineptitude, public failure, and emotional breakdowns are aired for the world to see, and we who peer into that "reality" can come away with a sense of superiority.

Dr. Jim Taylor made this observation:

TV has become the public executions of our times. We sit on the edge of our seats waiting eagerly for the guillotine to fall, yet don't want the end to come too quickly. . . . In these times of economic and global uncertainty, thanks to the contestants' symbolic deaths on reality TV, we can return to our lives feeling somehow better, safer . . . that we are going to be okay.[3]

So the question is not, "Is reality TV affecting you?" Rather, the question is, "How can you equip yourself to respond to the impact that reality TV has on you and on the culture?"

Colossians 2:8 says, "See to it that no one takes you captive through hollow and deceptive philosophy, which depends on human tradition and the basic principles of this world rather than on Christ" (NIV).

> How can you equip yourself to respond to the impact that reality TV has on you and on the culture? >

As with any cultural influence, each one of us must decide how we will respond. There are three likely responses—and you can undoubtedly figure out which one probably describes what Jesus' response would have been had there been reality TV in the first century.

1. **Hide:** One option is to act as though reality TV doesn't exist and therefore cannot have an effect on you. This approach considers cultural influences evil and believes that views and behaviors will rub off on us if we get too close. This approach, however, eliminates the need for discernment—and the ability to discern is a crucial skill for a believer. Certainly in specific instances the wisest choice is not to watch. However, being aware of our culture without being sucked in or fooled by it can enable us to have meaningful and productive conversations that lead to an opportunity to share the gospel.

2. **Join:** Another response to reality TV is to be so enchanted that we try to become like the people we see. Since surveys indicate that reality TV shows present bad behavior as acceptable, emulating what we see would certainly prove destructive. Jesus called us to be the difference in the world (Matthew 5:14–16). If our response to the influence of culture is to join in just as the world around us does, we won't be shining a light in the darkness.

3. **Engage:** Third, believers can be aware of the depravity seen on TV and then choose to address it with the love of Jesus. Instead of feeling insulted and disgusted, instead of hiding, believers should—as mentioned at point #1 above—engage others in conversations that could potentially lead to the gospel, just as Paul demonstrated in Acts 17:16–31.

If, for example, your friends are talking about how one houseguest flipped out on *Big Brother*, you might participate in the conversation by asking, "What do you think might have happened in her real life that caused her to lash out that way?" This simple question may lead to a discussion about searching for peace, hope, and joy. Of course, we know that the only true source of these is Jesus.

Bottom line, all of us today need to let God teach us how to approach reality TV—and our culture in general—by allowing our relationship with God to be our filter. Believers who understand that open doors to conversation await will engage the culture, rather than hide from it or join with it. And remember that by following the example of Paul, adopting the attitude of Jesus, and relying on the power of the Holy Spirit, you can harness even something completely secular for the purpose of the gospel.

Movies, TV, Music, Internet: How Much Is Too Much?

DR. JAY L. SEDWICK
Dallas Theological Seminary, Dallas, TX

What technology has become part of your everyday life? How many hours a day would you say you're using media? Keep your answers in mind as you read the following.

Every five years the Kaiser Family Foundation conducts a nationwide study of media usage by eight- to eighteen-year-olds. Their latest report from 2010 revealed some startling information about our involvement with (our addiction to?) technological devices: TV, music/audio, computer, video games, print, and movies. *Total Media Exposure* is the total time a person spends in a given day using all media—and that was 10 hours and 45 minutes per day. Kaiser then subtracted a multitasking proportion of 29 percent, the amount of time spent using more than one medium concurrently, to arrive at *Total Media Use*, which was 7 hours and 38 minutes per day—and that number didn't include the additional 1 hour and 35 minutes spent texting each day! (Are you using media or texting that much?) In Kaiser's 2005 report, *Total Media Use* was 6 hours and 21 minutes. The 1 hour and 17 minute daily increase in *Total Media Use* over the five years since their previous study was unexpected since that number had not shifted in the previous fifteen years. What caused this marked increase?

The Kaiser Family Foundation is convinced that the explosion of mobile and online media has fueled this increase in media use among young people. Ownership of mobile media devices has surged: 78 percent of eight- to eighteen-year-olds own an MP3 player or iPod; 66 percent own a cell phone; and 29 percent own a laptop. With smartphone sales setting records each quarter, these numbers are sure to continue growing.

Now, media itself is value neutral: there is nothing inherently bad or good about TV or the Internet. It's what peo-

> **It's what people do with media that makes it bad or good.** >

ple do with media that makes it bad or good. For instance, the pornography industry made billions using videotape and the VCR, and now the industry is exploiting the Internet for profits. By contrast, ministries all over the world have shown the *Jesus Film* on videotape to multiplied millions, leading to countless salvation decisions for Christ. The Hope Project by Mars Hill Productions, which tells the story of God's redemption of man from Genesis to Revelation, is free on the Internet and available in over forty languages. Whichever way it is used, media can be very influential, shaping lives and even entire cultures. Is media use more of a positive influence or a negative influence in your life?

The pervasive use of personal media devices, however, is creating new issues that may have an effect on developing a healthy Christian life. Numerous research studies show a relationship between social media usage, like Facebook and Twitter, and increased narcissism among users. The apostle Paul warned us about thinking too highly of ourselves: "Let nothing be done through selfish ambition or conceit, but in lowliness of mind let each esteem others better than himself. Let each of you look out not only for his own interests, but also for the interests of others" (Philippians 2:3–4) and "I say, through the grace given to me, to everyone who is among you, not to think of himself more highly than he ought to think, but to think soberly, as God has dealt to each one a measure of faith" (Romans 12:3). The apostle was encouraging every believer to exercise his or her spiritual gifts in the church, and humility—putting others first—rather than an inflated view of oneself is what fuels a desire to serve. (Have you seen social media increase narcissism?)

Research has also indicated that periods of solitude, silence, and reflection in the Christian life are affected by what one scholar has called *continuous partial attention* (CPA), which is defined as "paying partial attention continuously." CPA is driven by the desire to connect and to be connected all the time. People use their personal media devices to constantly stay connected to one another and to the world, because to be connected is to be alive. No wonder some media users avoid at all costs being disconnected from technology! This perspective, however, can undermine the spiritual disciplines of meditating on Scripture (Joshua 1:8; Psalm 1:2); spending time alone with God as Jesus did (Matthew 14:23; Mark 1:35); and reflecting on the things of God (Philippians 4:8; Colossians 3:1–2). Constant connectedness also affects one's ability to pay attention and focus. Attention spans seem to be shrinking among consistent media device users. Shorter attention spans mean an inability to attend to important experiences necessary for becoming more like Christ. Have you noticed your own attention span shrinking?

So what can you do to control media's influence in your life? Try taking a regular technology sabbatical, a break from using some or all of the media sources you regularly access. Put your smartphone away. Refrain from posting on Facebook or even checking your account for a period of time. Use some of that time to be alone with God, study His Word, and listen for His still small voice. If that possibility sounds impossible, your media may have become too important to you. Anything that gets in the way of your relationship with God is an idol and should be dealt with decisively.

With the TV, the Internet, movies, or a smartphone, the opportunity to consume inappropriate media—or an inappropriate amount of media—abounds. Make a promise to God that you will diligently seek Him. And call on Him to help you resist the temptation to participate in anything that does not lead you closer to Him.

In the World, but Not of It

STEVE BROWNING
Hebron Baptist Church, Dacula, GA

When I was in college, some friends and I visited the mountain city of Caracas, Venezuela, and decided to hike to the summit of one of those majestic peaks. With a local guide but not a lot of common sense, we set out to conquer the mountain. Being young and invincible, we paid little attention to the edge of the path and the steep drop. As I walked, talked, and laughed, I failed to notice how the path varied from wide to narrow.

In an instant, I stepped too close to the edge. The dry earth under my feet crumbled. I tumbled to the side and plunged off the path. Luckily, I got tangled in some brush, but I found myself dangling helplessly, head down, my ankles in the air. Quickly, my friends grabbed my feet and pulled me to safety. I was shaken, but okay . . .

One of the greatest issues facing you, the next generation of leaders, is making an impact on culture. Like the mountains of Venezuela, the culture can be very difficult to navigate. Culture changes the way we dress and talk. Culture dictates where we shop and what we buy. Culture defines *cool*, and often culture provides a misguided framework for how we are supposed to live. The power of culture's massive influence can be as intimidating as any mountain peak.

So should you simply not interact with culture? You know that our culture hardly embraces Christian values; our culture isn't gentle with believers. Do you worry that you will get pulled away from the foundation of your faith? Have you had people tell you to stay as far removed from culture as possible? You may have been instructed to, like refugees on the run, flee from the world you live in.

But is that how Jesus intended for you and me to live? In John 17, Jesus prayed for His disciples and those who would believe in Him in the future. He prayed, "I do not pray that You should take them out of the world, but that You should keep them from the evil one" (v. 15). You see, God never intended His people to run from culture. Instead, we are to do what Jesus modeled: we are to actively engage the culture in order to influence it for the better. John 1:14 describes Jesus as coming into the world and interacting with it in grace and truth. Though culture can be overwhelming, we are still called to engage it.

> We are to actively engage the culture in order to influence it for the better. **>**

Yet at the same time we need safeguards in our lives so we won't be negatively impacted by today's culture. Romans 12:2 instructs, "Do not be conformed to this world, but be transformed by the renewing of your mind." So how do we keep from being conformed to the very culture we live in and want to change?

1. **Live in relationship with fellow believers.** Clearly, I would have been in big trouble if I hadn't had friends with me on that Peruvian mountainside. But because they were there when I fell, they could help me get up before disaster happened. Keep that image in mind, because as we interact with the world we live in, we need strong Christian friends who are willing to keep us on track and help us when we stumble.

2. **Stay aware.** First Peter 5:8 says, "Be vigilant; because your adversary the devil walks about like a roaring lion, seeking whom he may devour." As we engage culture, we have to be aware of the enemy's traps. I fell off the mountain because I was unaware of the terrain. In this world, we can't

afford to be unaware of the cultural terrain. We have to see the spiritual pitfalls surrounding us as we both live in and interact with the world.

When we engage culture *and* guard our hearts against the enemy's attack, we will be able to stand firm in this generation and, as God's light and by His grace, make a differ-ence. Who knows? Maybe your generation will be the one to turn our culture and this world toward God.

> We need strong Christian friends who are willing to keep us on track and help us when we stumble. **>**

So engage the culture around you in the power of Jesus Christ and with His truth. And pray that God will use you: *Father, use me to make a difference in my generation, the culture, and the world so others may know You.*

Coarse, Crass, and Offensive

DR. JAY L. SEDWICK
Dallas Theological Seminary, Dallas, TX

"People judge you by the words you use." Verbal Advantage, a popular vocabulary building program, used that line in their television commercials to help convince people they needed to speak more intelligently in order to succeed in life. What comes out of your mouth when you speak really does matter, probably more than you realize. Abraham Lincoln once said, "It is better to remain silent and be thought a fool than to open one's mouth and remove all doubt."

It is one thing to say something that reveals a lack of understanding or information, but it is quite another to say something intentionally vulgar, gross, offensive, or profane. The use of profanity, however, is as old as language itself. The word *profane* comes from the Latin *profanus*, meaning "outside the temple." That which was located inside the Jewish temple in Jerusalem was considered holy, set apart for God's purposes. Everything outside the temple was not holy. Certain language today would never be allowed in the temple!

Our culture seems to be witnessing a steady increase in the use of coarse, crass, and offensive language, though. The Parent Television Council reported a 69 percent increase in the use of profanity across all television networks from 2005–2010. After peaking in 2008, Facebook and Twitter have actually seen a drop in the use of specific words considered profane. But don't be impressed. Social media users are now substituting acronyms for foul language rather than spelling out the words.

So is it wrong for Christians to use profanity? Is it wrong for Christians to use acronyms that represent profanity in their social media posts? Does the

Bible have anything to say about this? Last question first: yes, in fact, the Bible does have something to say.

Turn to Ephesians where Paul addressed a number of behavioral issues. Apparently, those believers—like many Christians today—struggled to control their speech. In Ephesians 4:29, Paul wrote, "Let no corrupt word proceed out of your mouth, but what is good for necessary edification, that it may impart grace to the hearers." The Greek word translated *corrupt* literally means "rotten." Clearly, we Christians should be careful to not speak rotten words.

Paul had a message for the believers at Colossae similar to the one he had sent to Ephesus. Concerned that they were still practicing their old evil ways, Paul exhorted them to "put off all these: anger, wrath, malice, blasphemy, filthy language out of your mouth" (Colossians 3:8). The imagery is that of throwing off a dirty shirt. In other words, believers should get rid of their filthy language.

Another biblical image representing speech is the tongue. James, the brother of Jesus, discussed an

> Our relationship with God is ineffectual if we don't control our speech. >

uncontrolled tongue in his letter to the first-century church: "If anyone among you thinks he is religious, and does not bridle his tongue but deceives his own heart, this one's religion is useless" (James 1:26). This strong statement tells us that our relationship with God is ineffectual if we don't control our speech. Using rhetorical questions, James then pointed out the contradiction of blessing and cursing coming out of the same mouth: How could fresh and bitter water come out of the same fountain? How could a fig tree grow olives or a grapevine bear figs? (James 3:10–12). These things are impossible. So it should be with Christians: cursing should not come out of our mouth. The words we say should represent the nature of who we are, and if we are Christians, then the Spirit of God should control our words.

Jesus also warned His hearers about the words they spoke: "Out of the abundance of the heart the mouth speaks. A good man out of the good treasure of his heart brings forth good things, and an evil man out of the evil treasure brings forth evil things. But I say to you that for every idle word men may speak, they will give account of it in the day of judgment" (Matthew 12:34–36). In other words, the things that we say, even carelessly, reveal what is in our hearts. A habit of swearing or using vulgar language reflects the way you think in your spirit—and God remembers every word you say. That fact alone should cause you to think twice before you speak.

If you struggle to control your language, either spoken aloud or keyed in cryptic acronyms, find someone to hold you accountable and pray for you. Paul knew the value of submitting to the wisdom and leadership of older believers in order to learn proper conduct (Titus 2:1–8). One skill more mature believers can mentor others in "sound speech that cannot be condemned" (Titus 2:8). There should be a clear and distinct difference between the way a Christian speaks and the way a non-Christian speaks. Do the words you use open you up to criticism and derision as a hypocrite? Is your ability to tell others about the change Christ can bring to a new believer's life hampered by a lack of change in this aspect of your own life?

As a Christian, you are responsible—24/7—for representing Christ as His ambassador (2 Corinthians 5:17–20). People will judge not only you by the words you use but also the One you represent. So "let your speech always be with grace, seasoned with salt, that you may know how you ought to answer each one" (Colossians 4:6).

Commit your speech to the Lord and ask Him to help you learn to control your tongue so that you will represent Christ well in all you say and do.

Help Stop the Epidemic

JOHN LEATHERS
First Baptist North Spartanburg, Spartanburg, SC

G ossip has become an epidemic, and it's ruining teenage relationships every day. You find gossip in the halls at school, in the break room at work, and even in the small groups at church. And gossip is spread through social media today, making the impact of such talk harder to avoid. Is there a remedy for this? Is there something we, as followers of Christ, can do to slow down this disease that destroys lives on a daily basis? Should we just stop talking and texting and simply communicate with grunts and body language? No, we must communicate. As followers of Christ, we just need to work on *how* we communicate—and gossip is one way we should *not* communicate.

Oxforddictionaries.com defines *gossip* as "casual or unconstrained conversation or reports about other people, typically involving details that are not confirmed as being true." I would like to add to the definition "sharing informa-

> As a follower of Christ, you have been set apart, which means your words, attitudes, and actions should be set apart as well. >

tion about somebody else without that person's permission." As we look at this definition, the phrase "not confirmed as being true" jumps out at me. Christian, you should never say something that is untrue. Remember the ninth commandment: "Thou shall not lie." We read the same in Colossians 3:9. So, as followers of Christ, we need to restrain from sharing untruths about others just so we can feel important or gain acceptance into a peer group. As a follower of

Christ, you have been set apart, which means your words, attitudes, and actions should be set apart as well. How, then, should you respond when you have the opportunity to share gossip or to hear gossip?

Let's talk first about sharing information. First and foremost, has the person given you permission to share this information that he or she has entrusted to you? If not, then you should not share. If you are not sure, then you should not share. If that person has given you permission, then share the truth. Don't embellish, trying to make the story sound more dramatic or funnier. Simply tell the truth, because Scripture is very vivid in its description of what happens when one gossips: "A gossip betrays a confidence; so avoid a man who talks too much" (Proverbs 20:19 NIV). Proverbs 16:28 tells us that "gossip separates close friends" (NIV). Students, if you want to end a relationship, the quickest way to do this is by gossiping. So if you have a tough time bridling your tongue, then maybe you should do what Scripture says and avoid people who talk too much. Stay away from situations where you would hear information that you know you shouldn't share. The less information you have on others, the less you will share.

And what if you find yourself on the receiving end of information that you believe to be untrue? How many of you, for instance, have ever been involved in gossip disguised as a prayer request? (Remember, don't lie!) We've all been there. It happens at the conclusion of a small-group meeting or a Sunday school class. You're going around the room taking prayer requests, and you come to that one student who says, "I probably shouldn't say this, but I really feel this person needs our prayers." And then all the details come flowing out.

> How many of you have ever been involved in gossip disguised as a prayer request? >

As a follower of Christ, you must stop the gossip before it starts. Whether in a setting like this or in the lunchroom at school, you need to firmly but kindly say to the one gossiping, "I would prefer to hear this information from the person himself/herself rather than from you." This same principle applies to Facebook. If you discover that one of your friends is constantly gossiping, first confront that friend in love. If that doesn't make a difference, de-friend him or her. When it comes to sharing information on the Internet or in a tweet, writing something that is untrue or something you were not given permission to share is just as bad as saying it. Actually, it's much worse, because not just one person or a handful will hear it; thousands could read it. Besides, Scripture tells us to build one another up and to encourage one another. Gossip never builds up another person; gossip is never encouraging.

As followers of Christ, we are called to "walk worthy of the Lord, fully pleasing Him, being fruitful in every good work" (Colossians 1:10). Let this be the desire that guides you . . . and your words.

#random stuff

The Truth of Scripture

> DR. JAY STRACK
> Student Leadership University, Orlando, FL

Has the quest for truth been replaced by an insatiable appetite for opinion? Consider that an Internet search for *blog* brings up 11 trillion, 920 million–plus related sites offering unsolicited opinions. Also, in a single twelve-month period, the number of tweets per day doubled from 200 million to 400 million, and that number continues to grow. These blogs and tweets are random thoughts, thrown into the universe, for anyone to consider.

Against the background of all those words and ideas flying around, truth can easily get lost or overlooked. *But,* our postmodern society wonders, *does truth even exist?* Some people today believe truth is defined in the same way a fantasy football team is created: pick and choose team members, discard or exchange at will. Yet truth (lowercase *t*) is defined as "the state of being the case, an original or standard."[1] Truth is reliable and inflexible; it will not change with the passage of time or in the face of opposing opinions, new circumstances, or cultural trends. And in our hearts is a longing for truth; a thirst for what is good, real, and steadfast.

Thankfully that thirst can be fully satisfied. In fact, for millennia we've had the ability to satisfy our thirst for truth. I'm talking about the Bible, literally the Book of Books, which declares itself to be Truth (capital *T*). And Jesus Himself, the One who is the Way, the Truth, and the Life, supports the Bible's assertion by fulfilling Old Testament prophecies centuries after they were written (John 14:6).

The Bible is basically a library of sixty-six books . . . written in three different languages . . . by more than forty people . . . from all walks of life . . . over a period of more than one thousand years . . . and the content covers a wide variety of ancient peoples and cultures.[2] The central story of the Bible's Grand

Narrative, however, is the unveiling of our very real God and His involvement in the world He created. The Bible also tells the good, the bad, and the ugly about humanity.

In our enemy's first interaction with the creation God made in His image—Adam and Eve—Satan attempted to distort Truth, and it worked. In Genesis 3:1 (NIV), Satan asked Eve, "Did God *really* say . . . ?" Confused and curious, she accepted this distorted representation of God's Word and made a decision that has affected all mankind. The deceiver's method has not changed. He continues to tempt us to alter God's Word to fit a given situation or desire. Don't do it.

But back to the Bible: it is God's story. And that story has been described this way: "Behind 10,000 events stands God, the builder of history, the maker of the ages. Eternity bounds the one side, eternity bounds the other side, and time is in between: Genesis-origins. Revelation-endings, and all the way between, God is working things out."[3]

> **The Bible is God's story.** >

* The Bible tells us "no prophecy of Scripture is of any private interpretation, for prophecy never came by the will of man, but holy men of God spoke as they were moved by the Holy Spirit" (2 Peter 1:20–21).
* The accuracy of facts and the fulfillment of prophecies in the Bible testify to its Truth.
* Eyewitnesses wrote the following:
  * "That . . . which we have heard, which we have seen with our eyes, which we have looked upon, and our hands have handled, concerning the Word of life—the life was manifested, and we have seen, and bear witness, and declare to you that eternal life which was with the Father and was manifested to us" (1 John 1:1–2).
  * "We . . . were eyewitnesses of His majesty" (2 Peter 1:16).

* Jesus fulfilled many prophecies of the Old Testament, including these:

- The Messiah would be born of a virgin (Isaiah 7:14) in Bethlehem (Micah 5:2).
- The Messiah would be mocked and ridiculed, pierced in hands and feet (Psalm 22).

Many other biblical prophecies have come to pass, and many historical documents support biblical accounts as fact, including Christ's resurrection and His miracles. Therefore, at some point every person must decide for himself or herself whether to accept the Word of God as the absolute authority in their personal choices.

We have yet one more witness to the Truth of the Bible, and that is the Holy Spirit who comes to live within us when we receive the gift of salvation through Christ Jesus. Also called the Spirit of Truth, He came to us directly from the Lord Jesus: "The Helper, the Holy Spirit, whom the Father will send in My name, He will teach you all things, and bring to your remembrance all things that I said to you" (John 14:26). Now how is that for one-to-one tutoring!

> At some point every person must decide for himself or herself whether to accept the Word of God as the absolute authority in their personal choices. **>**

This Word of God is powerful and living: That is, it continues to apply to every life in every situation for every time in history: "The word of God is living and powerful, and sharper than any two-edged sword" (Hebrews 4:12).

God's Word is able to bring salvation: "From childhood you have known the Holy Scriptures, which are able to make you wise for salvation through faith which is in Christ Jesus" (2 Timothy 3:15).

The Word of God leads us to a grand future: "All Scripture is given by inspiration of God, and is profitable for doctrine, for reproof, for correction, for instruction in righteousness, that the man of God may be complete, thoroughly equipped for every good work" (2 Timothy 3:16–17).

I believe everything this Book says, from Genesis to Revelation, not only for the reasons mentioned above, but because Jesus has come into my life in a powerful, life-transforming way. Daily He lives within me, calling me to Himself and to His Word. I believe in absolute Truth.

Is There Really a Hell?

> MATT RODEN
> The People's Church, Spring Hill, TN

Here are some things you just don't mention in certain settings. You never mention politics at Christmas dinner. You never vividly describe how attractive your date is . . . to her parents. And you never mention the subject of hell around . . . well, around anyone. Christian or not, everyone has strong feelings about hell. Some feel that it is impossible for a loving God to send anyone to hell. Others feel that the whole world (except for them, of course) is headed to hell in a hurry. Whatever our emotions, the question remains: Does hell really exist?

Recent studies have found that most Americans struggle with whether or not hell exists. While 91 percent of Americans believe heaven exists, only 74 percent believe hell exists.[1] The problem with hell does not seem to be that it *could* exist, but whether it *should* exist at all. The Bible says that God is love (1 John 4:8). So how can a loving God send His own people and even *good* people—each one of whom He created—to any type of eternal punishment?

But there are *other* parts of the Bible, and its many passages about hell not only raise our eyebrows but may also give us chills. Take 2 Thessalonians 1:7–9, for example:

> You who are suffering, God will give you rest along with us when the Lord Jesus appears suddenly from heaven in flaming fire with his mighty angels, bringing judgment on those who do not wish to know God and who refuse to accept his plan to save them through our Lord Jesus Christ. They will be punished in everlasting hell, forever separated from the Lord, never to see the glory of his power. (TLB)

Where did the *loving* God go? In this passage, we see Jesus ripping through the skies in a massive blaze of fire with an army of angels. He brings judgment on those who denied God and refused Christ, and they are punished in everlasting hell. This passage leaves no doubt: an eternal separation from God, an everlasting destruction, awaits those who reject His love. But if God *is* love, then how is this even possible?

You could stop here, form your own opinions about God, and move on. But without diving deeper into this issue, we cast God aside as double-minded and completely miss the point. Further exploration reveals a heartbreaking tragedy that is widely misinterpreted. Hell is not something that God ever intended for us. Hell is something we demanded. I'll explain.

> Hell is not something that God ever intended for us. Hell is something we demanded. **>**

To understand the existence of hell, we must remember that God gives all human beings the ability to choose. All of us can either love God or reject Him. God established this in the very beginning when He created the first man and first woman (Genesis 2–3). He did not program them to love Him: they were not mindless robots forever set on worship mode. God gave them total freedom to love Him or reject Him. God did so by planting a tree in the middle of the garden and telling them that eating the fruit of that tree would result in death. They could love God and honor His commands, or they could reject Him and take the fruit. Later, with the help of a certain serpent, Adam and Eve chose to reject God's plan for them. We still feel the consequences of their decision.

But back to this issue of love and choice. You cannot have real love without choice. Real love is not overriding someone's will so he or she will love you. Real love only exists if someone chooses to love you. God gives us all the freedom to be with Him or be without Him. We can be with Him and experience

His forgiveness and power in our lives. Or we can choose to be without Him, carve our own way through life, and live with the consequences. God will give us every opportunity possible to love Him and accept what He did for us through Christ. But when our lives are over, God gives us what we wanted: He gives us what we chose.

Those who have lived out a lifelong rejection of God are not going to be forced to be with Him or love Him. In the end, God will honor what they have chosen: an eternity without Him. They rejected and refused His love up to their dying breath, and God will grant them their wish that He would leave them alone.

Hell is not a place created as some sort of morbid punishment because God has an ego problem. Hell is the natural result of a person's lifelong choice to be separated from God. Hell is the tragic end to a story of unrequited love. Hell is the eternal separation from love that follows a life that consistently rejected that love. God does not override our wills in this life, and He doesn't after death. God gives us every chance possible to find love and salvation, and He honors our ultimate decision.

Interpreted out of context, the flames and agony of hell described in the Bible could paint God as sadistic. But hell is far more a commentary about us than it is about God. After all, God loves us enough to give us a choice.

The existence of hell and the reasons for its existence cause us to realize that our lives here truly matter. The choices we make and even the conversations we have will echo in eternity. Many Bible passages speak of hell, and many other questions could be asked and discussions had, but the significance of rejecting God's love for us is too large to ignore. Our refusal to give our hearts to God is a choice that affects everything. Hell is an undeniable reality, but—by God's grace—a completely avoidable destination.

Does Paranormal Activity Exist?

MATT RODEN
The People's Church, Spring Hill, TN

You're home alone. Everything is fine. Then you hear something. Maybe a loud thump or a creaking door, and suddenly you've gone from fine to frightened. You slowly move toward the noise. Then you see it . . . It's the cat, and you breathe a sigh of relief.

Through the years, a great number of movies and TV shows have attempted to frighten us with monsters, zombies, vampires, demons, and ghosts. (Even in Jesus' day people thought ghosts were real [Luke 24:37–39], but the Bible does not confirm the existence of ghosts or any other supernatural beings.) Entertainment has made it difficult to separate *real* evil from wild imaginings. Even Christians are unsure what is fact and what is fiction. One study found that 59 percent of Christians believe Satan is *not* a real living being, but merely a symbol of evil. Yet 64 percent still believe that a person can be influenced by forces of evil. Researcher George Barna made this comment: "Hollywood has made evil accessible and tame, making Satan and demons less worrisome than the Bible suggests they really are. It's hard for achievement-driven, self-reliant, independent people to believe that their lives can be impacted by unseen forces."[1]

So is there a real evil out there? The Bible gives us this snapshot of the dark side of the supernatural: "We are not fighting against flesh-and-blood enemies, but against evil rulers and authorities of the unseen world, against mighty powers in this dark world, and against evil spirits in the heavenly places" (Ephesians 6:12 NLT). Here the Bible describes a demonic presence that is everywhere, well organized, and totally against us.

But what are demons doing and what do they want? To understand evil, you have to understand its origin. First of all, the Bible is clear: Satan is an actual living being with a tragic history and furiously destructive ambition. His backstory is scattered throughout the Bible.[2] When the pieces are put together, the account cannot be ignored. Here's the short version:

Before God made humans, he made angels. They, like us, have the ability to choose whether or not to love God. The chief angel, named Lucifer (which means "bright star"), was mesmerizingly beautiful. His beauty and glory caused pride to overtake him, so instead of simply being *with* God, Lucifer decided he would rather *be* God. He rebelled against God and led other angels to rebel as well. God quickly ended the rebellion by throwing Lucifer and his followers out of heaven and onto earth. Then God created man in His own image and gave us dominion over the earth (a new chief!).

If you can't destroy Someone, the next best tactic is to destroy what He loves. Lucifer knew he couldn't destroy God, but he could cause this new creation to join in his rebellion against Him. So when the man and woman were in the garden of Eden, Lucifer appeared in disguise and lured them into making a fatal mistake (Genesis 3). After that, the Bible referred to Lucifer as *Satan*, which means "accuser." He tried to ruin Job's life, tempted Jesus in the wilderness, and seeks to move our hearts away from God. So the Bible warns us: "Be vigilant; because your adversary the devil walks about like a roaring lion, seeking whom he may devour" (1 Peter 5:8). Satan and demons (the angels that fell with him) are real, living beings determined to steal, kill, and destroy (John 10:10). So how should we respond?

There are two terrible ways to respond. The first is to pretend Satan and demons are not real and ignore the issue. The second is to try to mix the biblical view of Satan and demons with Hollywood versions where every creaking door and flickering light is seen as the work of a demon. The first response denies the reality of evil; the second response sees evil in everything. But the fact is that Satan is less interested in turning your lights on and off than he is in turning your life off the path God has for you.

The Bible has one singular response to real evil—and it may surprise you:

- Put on every piece of God's armor so you will be able to resist the enemy. . . .
- Then after the battle you will still be standing firm. (Ephesians 6:13 NLT)
- Stand firm against [the devil], and be strong in your faith. (1 Peter 5:9 NLT)
- Resist the devil and he will flee from you. (James 4:7)
- God has not given us a spirit of fear, but of power and of love and of a sound mind. (2 Timothy 1:7)

The Bible makes it clear that evil is not something to fear, but something to fight. Christ has authority over everything, and He lives in those who believe in Him. So we have incredible authority and power over evil because of Christ. Again, evil is nothing to fear; it is something we are charged to fight.

Yet the entertainment world usually portrays evil as an unstoppable force, something almost undefeatable. But real evil, according to the Bible, is very stoppable and can be defeated. When Christ interacted with demons, He had no fear at all. They wanted to get away from Him, though (Matthew 8:31; Mark 1:34; 5:10–12; Luke 4:41; 10:17). The Bible says that demons tremble when they think about God (James 2:19). In reality, demonic evil is simply not as impressive as the Hollywood versions.

> Evil is not something to fear, but something to fight. **>**

But what was that noise? Probably just a noise. Remember that there are more tricks about the supernatural than truth out there. Does the supernatural exist? Sure. The Bible confirms that real angels, real demons, and a real Satan truly exist. The ghosts, vampires, and the rest are just stories.

Hope for Freedom

SHAUN BLAKENEY
Christ Fellowship, Palm Beach Gardens, FL

Human trafficking is modern-day slavery—and it's the fastest growing criminal industry in the world. This industry includes the recruitment, transportation, harboring, and taking of persons by means of threat, force, bullying, abduction, fraud, or deception for the purpose of abusing them.

The United Nations estimates that around the world 2.5 million people are trafficked annually. Victims of trafficking are forced into employment or sexual exploitation. Labor trafficking ranges from domestic service in small operations to large-scale operations such as farms, sweatshops, and major multinational corporations.

Labor trafficking is vast, but sex trafficking is one of the most profitable forms of trafficking. It involves any form of sexual abuse in prostitution, pornography, and the commercial sexual abuse of children. Sex trafficking robs people of their human rights and freedoms, it is a global health risk, it fuels organized crime, and it is wrong.

And human trafficking is not just happening in other countries; it's also happening in the United States. An estimated three hundred thousand American children are at risk for trafficking into the sex industry every year.

Here are some hard facts about the all-too-real scourge of human trafficking:

* 27 million people are enslaved worldwide, 50 percent are children, and some are sold for as little as twenty dollars.
* Every thirty seconds, another person becomes a victim of trafficking.
* The average age of girls enslaved is twelve to fourteen.
* 99 percent of the victims are never rescued.

These statistics are staggering, and these crimes should prompt all of us to act. After all, God has a high regard for human life. The Bible teaches that when God created humans, He created them in His image:

> God said, "Let us make human beings in our image, to be like us. They will reign over the fish in the sea, the birds in the sky, the livestock, all the wild animals on the earth, and the small animals that scurry along the ground." (Genesis 1:26 NLT)

God values everyone, every life has immeasurable value to Him, and He extends His unconditional love to everyone.

First John 4:8 says that God is love: "He who does not love does not know God, for God is love." Since we were created in the image of God, we were created to love.

In the New Testament, we read Jesus' command to "love your neighbor" (Matthew 19:19) and to help those in need (Luke 10:25–37). In addition, Proverbs 31:8–9 says, "Speak up for those who cannot speak for themselves; ensure justice for those being crushed. Yes, speak up for the poor and helpless, and see that they get justice" (NLT). These

> Every single one of us must *pray* for those who are enslaved in human trafficking. >

doctrines definitely apply to victims of the illegal practice of human trafficking.

So how can you and I put these biblical doctrines into practice and speak up for those affected by human trafficking and see that they get justice?

1. Every single one of us must *pray* for those who are enslaved in human trafficking. James 5:16 says, "The effective, fervent prayer of a righteous [person] avails much." To bring an end to human trafficking we must stand together in prayer. We must pray for freedom and expect

that God will deliver. It's only through His power that those who are enslaved in this industry will be released.

2. We have to speak out for those whose voices aren't able to be heard. Isaiah 1:17 says, "Learn to do good. Seek justice. Help the oppressed. Defend the cause of orphans. Fight for the rights of widows" (NLT). Although the crime of human trafficking is plaguing our world today, it is still too much in the shadows. Once we know about the injustice of this modern-day slavery, we must talk about it with our friends and in churches, schools, businesses, and communities. Stop and ask yourself if God is calling you to stand in the gap for those in slavery. Maybe God is asking you to be a voice of justice.

3. We must take action against human trafficking to help those who are enslaved. In the past couple of years, several organizations have arisen that are giving Christians opportunities to serve in the fight, and there are many options:

   * You can volunteer in an anti-trafficking group.
   * You can give financially to organizations that are working to put an end to slavery.
   * You can continue to educate yourself in human trafficking and begin to lead a movement in your community to end this modern-day slavery.

4. A very easy, practical way to help in the fight against human trafficking is by supporting fair trade goods. These products are made and sold by companies that strive for just and safe working environments; they don't employ slaves. Look for fair trade teas, chocolate, and coffee.

Human trafficking is an injustice against men, women, and children. Every human is made in the image of God and created to live not in slavery, but in freedom. We are called to not just read the Word of God, but also be doers of the Word (James 1:22). As doers of the Word we should be praying, speaking out against modern-day slavery, and doing what we can to help bring light to the darkness.

> Human trafficking is an injustice against men, women, and children. >

Will you embrace Christ, share His message of freedom, and become part of a generation of outspoken warriors impacting this world and releasing the chains of oppression?

Spiritual Poverty in an Affluent Culture

CHRISTIAN NICHLES
First Baptist Church Midland, Midland, TX

"Blessed are the poor in spirit, for theirs is the kingdom of heaven."

—Jesus in Matthew 5:3

I f you have the ability and the means to read this, you are among the small percentage of people on Planet Earth entrusted with affluence. Although the numbers often vary from one organization to another, the facts are pretty well known: most of the world does not live in a lavish subdivision populated by well-educated adults or with #firstworldprobz trending on their Twitter feed. Your generation stands in a unique place in world history: you may become the most impoverished wealthy generation ever. *But how,* you ask, *can wealth and poverty coexist?* The ugly truth is that the only way one exists is because of the other: they are apparent opposites that inevitably attract.

> Your generation may become the most impoverished wealthy generation ever. **>**

First, what do the terms *poverty* and *affluence* even mean? According to the *Cambridge Dictionary, affluence* means "having a lot of money or possessions; rich." *Poverty*, on the other hand, is defined as "the condition of being poor." When we begin to think about your generation's affluence, it is astounding. Your access to and use of technology, the bombardment of fashion and style, the ability to travel, the level of education available—I could go on and on. The fact is, even though huge numbers of people live in poverty, the wealth and affluence of the minority is actually, in sum total, larger than the poverty that exists. Let me explain.

Did you know that Americans spent $54 billion on a recent Black Friday weekend?[1] Here's why that statistic matters. According to the World Bank, "The cost of reaching 'basic levels of coverage . . . in water and sanitation' [is estimated] to be $9 billion at the low end, and $30 billion a year for 'achieving universal coverage' for water and sanitation. Taking these estimates and their caveats together, we estimate that the cost . . . is between $5 and $21 billion."[2] Are you kidding me? If we simply spent half of what we spend on Christmas and gave the other half to God's kingdom efforts, we could solve the world's water crisis? Then why don't we? Often we don't because we don't care about what Jesus cares about, and we can't know what Jesus cares about because we don't know Jesus. One of the most critical issues facing your generation, then, is moving past the "little Jesus in my pocket"[3] to a place of full surrender to the mighty King Jesus and His kingdom plans.

So when King Jesus addressed critical issues, He did so with poignant and purposeful dialogue. In the crowds that gathered, He saw the full range of socioeconomics, ethnicities, family dynamics, and spiritual traditions. In Matthew 5, for instance, Jesus recognized that some people in the crowd had many possessions but needed a greater purpose in life. Jesus also knew that if this group of people would embrace their need for Him and His kingdom, they would actually make a greater and more positive impact on the world than if they tried to leverage their own thoughts, ideas, and purposes. For those of us entrusted with this moment in history, the question is, "Will we embrace our need for Jesus and His kingdom agenda? Will we embrace our spiritual poverty?"

> Will we embrace our need for Jesus and His kingdom agenda? Will we embrace our spiritual poverty? >

In a culture that screams, "This world is about me! God most certainly exists for *my* benefit!"[4] how can we shift our position of affluence to a position of spiritual poverty that actually brings a wealth of benefit to the kingdom of God? First, we need to realize that *we have been placed in this time and this place for God's glory*, not for our own benefit. Recognizing the heavenly kingdom—ruled not by us, but by a glorious King who desires the very best for His people—will open our eyes to the kingdom distinctive of Jesus' call to the spiritually impoverished. This awareness of the spiritually poor will also help us engage in our calling to not only be citizens of this kingdom but also to be advocates for our King.

Second, we must acknowledge that *the king who rules my life is Jesus*, not me! We must embrace the true identity of the only Son of God as He rules supremely from His throne, and we must understand that He intends for His people to commit to the same kingdom values He has. We must choose this shift in thinking—from "Jesus as mascot" to "Jesus as Monarch"[5]—every day in order to live with the self-abandonment Jesus commanded of His disciples: "If anyone desires to come after Me, let him deny himself, and take up his cross daily, and follow Me" (Luke 9:23).

The last, but certainly not the least important point, the surrender of our self-reliance and affluence will bring us to the point of spiritual poverty necessary to see the great need for the world's people to become citizens of the kingdom of heaven.

The supreme King loves you and me and calls us to serve in His kingdom. Will you who are affluent answer His call, recognizing your spiritual poverty and letting Him use you for His kingdom purposes? Will you use all that God has entrusted to you to make a global impact for His eternal kingdom? You answer yes only by embracing and then living out John the Baptist's heart cry, "He must increase, but I must decrease" (John 3:30).

#endnotes

PERFECTIONISM: Living in a World That Demands Perfection
Jeremy Nottingham

1. Thom Rainer and Jess Rainer, *The Millennials* (Nashville, TN: Broadman & Holman Publishing, 2011), 22.
2. Ibid., 23.

SELF-ESTEEM: What We Should Say to Our Reflection
Brooke Cooney

1. J. Swanson and O. Nave, *New Nave's Topical Bible* (Oak Harbor, WA: Logos Research Systems, 1994).

PERSEVERANCE: The Quitting Complex *Dr. Jay Strack*

1. William Barclay, *Letters to the Philippians, Colossians, and Thessalonians*, 3rd ed. (Louisville, KY: Westminster John Knox, 2003), 83.

PEER PRESSURE: Who Am I? *Ron Cooney*

1. Charles R. Swindoll, *Tale of the Tardy Oxcart* (Nashville, TN: Thomas Nelson, 1998), 434.

ACCOUNTABILITY: Iron Sharpening Iron *Mike Calhoun*

1. http://ngm.nationalgeographic.com/2011/10/teenage-brains/dobbs-text/1.
2. http://www.psychologytoday.com/blog/trouble-in-mind/201112 /brilliant-brazen-teenage-brains.
3. http://www.npr.org/templates/story/story.php?storyId=124119468.

CYBERBULLYING: The Myth of Sticks and Stones *Shaun Blakeney*

1. http://www.cyberbullying.us/cyberbullying_fact_sheet.pdf.

SEX: What Does the Bible Really Say About Sex? *Dr. Danny Akin*

1. Peggy Fletcher Stack, "What They Didn't Teach You About Sex in Sunday School," *RNS*, October 13, 2000.

HOMOSEXUALITY: Born This Way *Ric Garland*

1. Charles Caldwell Ryrie, *A Survey of Bible Doctrine* (Chicago: Moody Press, 1972).

PORNOGRAPHY: It's a Brain Changer *Dennis Steeger*

1. William M. Struthers, *Wired for Intimacy: How Pornography Hijacks the Male Brain* (Sydney, AUST: ReadHowYouWant, 2012).
2. Ibid., 41.

PORNOGRAPHY: Far-Reaching Consequences *Ron Cooney*

1. Chiara Sabina, Janis Wolak, and David Finkelhor, "The Nature and Dynamics of Internet Pornography Exposure for Youth," in *CyberPsychology & Behavior*, December 2008: 691–93, accessed November 28, 2012, http://online.liebert-pub.com/toc/cpb/12/6.
2. Richard J. Foster, *Celebration of Discipline: The Path to Spiritual Growth* (San Francisco, CA: HarperOne, 1978), 5–6.

ABSENT PARENTS: Growing Up with Absent Parents
Jeremy Nottingham

1. Chap Clark, *Hurt: Inside the World of Today's Teenagers* (Grand Rapids, MI: Baker Academic, 2004), 49.

DEALING WITH LOSS: Facing Loss without Losing Faith

Mike Calhoun

1. A. W. Tozer, *The Knowledge of the Holy* (San Francisco, CA: HarperOne, 1978).

DEPRESSION: The Depression Epidemic *Ron Luce*

1. http://www.suicide.org.
2. Associated Press, January 11, 2010, "Study: Youth Now Have More Mental Health Issues," http://www.foxnews.com/story/0,2933,582742,00.html.

SUICIDE: If Life Is Getting Dark . . . for You or Someone You Know *Keith Harmon*

1. "Suicide Statistics," A Fierce Good-Bye: Living in the Shadow of Suicide, http://www.fiercegoodbye.com/?s=2, accessed on December 3, 2012. Compiled statistics from Suicidology.org website on survivors, Center for Disease Control, and National Institute of Mental Health, and from The Jason Foundation, Inc. See http://www.nimh.nih.gov/SuicidePrevention/suifact.cfm, http://www.cdc.gov/ncipc/factsheets/suifacts.htm, http://www.suicidology.org/displaycommon.cfm?an=1&subarticlwaenbr=21.

SEX: Taking Care of Your Temple *Jerry Pipes*

1. Zig Ziglar, "Get Motivated" seminar, Georgia Dome, Atlanta, GA, November 1, 2010.

ALCOHOL AND DRUGS: To Drink or Not to Drink? *Derek Simpson*

1. http://www.cdc.gov/media/releases/2011/p1017_alcohol_consumption.html.

A COMPARTMENTALIZED LIFE: Not Just on Sunday

Joseph McMurry

1. Mitch Kruse, "Compartmentalizing God" http://www.mitchkruse.com/pdf/compartmentalizing-god.pdf.

WALKING THE WALK: Starting Over—By God's Grace *Matt Petty*

1. Mark Batterson, *Primal: A Quest for the Lost Soul of Christianity* (Colorado Springs, CO: WaterBrook Multnomah, 2009).

LIVING WITH INTEGRITY: God's Guidelines for the Gray Areas of Life *Dr. Danny Akin*

1. John Piper, *Desiring God* (Sisters, OR: Multnomah, 1996), 9.

HONORING GOD: Dig Wells or Build Fences? *Brent Crowe*

1. Michael Frost and Alan Hirsch *The Shaping of Things to Come* (Peabody, MA: Hendrickson Publishers, 2003), 47.
2. Brent Crowe, *Chasing Elephants* (Colorado Springs, CO: NavPress, 2010), 76–85.

GOD'S CALL: Answering God's Callings *Brent Crowe*

1. Gene Edward Veith, *God at Work: Your Christian Vocation in All of Life* (Wheaton, IL: Crossway, 2002), 19.
2. Ibid., 39.

YOUNG LEADERS: Jesus Chose Who? *Chris White*

1. http://www.conservapedia.com/Great_Achievements_by_Teenagers.

SOCIAL MEDIA: Using Your Influence for Good *Brad Hobbs*

1. Tatiana Schlossberg, "Literacy Rates," *Timothy McSweeney's Internet Tendency*, accessed November 29, 2012, http://www.mcsweeneys.net/articles/literacy-rates.

TV: Culture and Reality TV *Joseph McMurry*

1. Girl Scout Research Institute, "Real to Me: Girls and Reality TV," 2011, http://www.girlscouts.org/research/publications/girlsandmedia/real_to_me.asp.

2. The National Center on Addiction and Substance Abuse at Columbia University, National Survey of American Attitudes on Substance Abuse XVI: Teens and Parents, 2011, http://www.casacolumbia.org/templates /NewsRoom.aspx?articleid=648&zoneid=51.
3. Jim Taylor, PhD, "The Cluttered Mind, Uncluttered," 2010, http://drjimtaylor.com/2.0/aboutdrjimtaylor/, http://blog.ctnews.com /taylor/about-dr-jim-taylor/.

INERRANCY: The Truth of Scripture *Dr. Jay Strack*

1. http://www.merriam-webster.com/dictionary/truth.
2. *The Chronological Guide to the Bible: Explore God's Word in Historical Order* (Nashville, TN: Thomas Nelson, 2010), Introduction.
3. Dr. Henrietta Mears, *What the Bible Is All About* (Ventura, CA: Regal, 2007), 13.

HELL: Is There Really a Hell? *Matt Roden*

1. http://www.foxnews.com/story/0,2933,173838,00.html.

PARANORMAL: Does Paranormal Activity Exist? *Matt Roden*

1. http://www.barna.org/barna-update/article/12-faithspirituality/260-most -american-christians-do-not-believe-that-satan-or-the-holy-spirit-exis.
2. Genesis 3; Job 1–2; Isaiah 14; Ezekiel 28; Matthew 4; Luke 10; 2 Peter 2; Jude 6; Revelation 12.

LIVING IN AFFLUENCE: Spiritual Poverty in an Affluent Culture *Christian Nichles*

1. http://money.cnn.com/2011/11/27/pf/black_friday/index.htm.
2. http://www.water.cc/water-crisis/related-news/.
3. Richard Ross, *Student Ministry and the Supremacy of Christ* (Bloomington, IN: Crossbooks, 2009).
4. A thought gleaned from reading page 6 of Ross's *Student Ministry* and the findings of research done by Christian Smith.
5. Ross, 7–8.

#contributors